The Growth of Early Old World Civilizations, *Robert M. Adams*

The Stages of Human Evolution: Human and Cultural Origins, *C. Loring Brace*

The Sub-Human Primates and Their Social Life, *Michael R. A. Chance and Clifford J. Jolly*

New World Prehistory: Archaeology of the American Indian, *William T. Sanders and Joseph J. Marino*

Linguistic Anthropology, *A. Richard Diebold, Jr.*

Ethnological Theory, *David Kaplan*

Formation of the State, *Lawrence Krader*

Tribesmen, *Marshall D. Sahlins*

The Hunters, *Elman R. Service*

Peasants, *Eric R. Wolf*

The Present as Anthropology, *Peter Worsley*

The Evolutionary Basis of Race, *Ernst Goldschmidt*

P R E N T I C E - H A L L , I N C . , *Englewood Cliffs, New Jersey*

WITHDRAWN

Marshall D. Sahlins, University of Michigan

Tribesmen

To My Parent

Frontispiece: The town of Secota (Secoton).

Theodore De Bry's engraving for his Virginia Volume,

issued in 1590, made after the watercolor by John White.

Designed by Harry Rinehart. Illustrated by BMA Associates.

PRENTICE-HAL

FOUNDATIONS OF MODERN ANTHROPOLOGY SERIE

Marshall D. Sahlins, *Edito*

Current printing (last digit):
10   9   8   7   6   5   4   3   2   1

PRENTICE-HALL INTERNATIONAL, INC., *London*

PRENTICE-HALL OF AUSTRALIA, PTY., LTD., *Sydney*

PRENTICE-HALL OF CANADA, LTD., *Toronto*

PRENTICE-HALL OF INDIA PVT. LTD., *New Delhi*

PRENTICE-HALL OF JAPAN, INC., *Tokyo*

Foundations

of Modern Anthropology

Series

The Foundations of Modern Anthropology Series is a documentation of the human condition, past and present. It is concerned mainly with exotic peoples, prehistoric times, unwritten languages, and unlikely customs. But this is merely the anthropologist's way of expressing his concern for the here and now, and his way makes a unique contribution to our knowledge of what's going on in the world. We cannot understand ourselves apart from an understanding of *man*, nor our culture apart from an understanding of *culture*. Inevitably we are impelled toward an intellectual encounter with man in all his varieties, no matter how primitive, how ancient, or how seemingly insignificant. Ever since their discovery by an expanding European civilization, primitive peoples have continued to hover over thoughtful men like ancestral ghosts, ever provoking this anthropological curiosity. To "return to the primitive" just for what it is would be foolish; the savage is not nature's nobleman and his existence is no halcyon idyll. For anthropology, the romance of the primitive has been something else:

v

a search for the roots and meaning of ourselves—in the context of all mankind.

The series, then, is designed to display the varieties of man and culture and the evolution of man and culture. All fields of anthropology are relevant to the grand design and all of them—prehistoric archaeology, physical anthropology, linguistics, and ethnology (cultural anthropology)—are represented among the authors of the several books in the series. In the area of physical anthropology are books describing the early condition of humanity and the subhuman primate antecedents. The later development of man on the biological side is set out in the volume on races, while the archaeological accounts of the Old World and the New document development on the historical side. Then there are the studies of contemporary culture, including a book on how to understand it all—i.e., on ethnological theory—and one on language, the peculiar human gift responsible for it all. Main types of culture are laid out in "The Hunters," "Tribesmen," "Formation of the State," and "Peasants." Initiating a dialogue between contemplation of the primitive and the present, the volume on "The Present as Anthropology" keeps faith with the promise of anthropological study stated long ago by E. B. Tylor, who saw in it "the means of understanding our own lives and our place in the world, vaguely and imperfectly it is true, but at any rate more clearly than any former generation."

Preface

Any selection of primitive societies for textbook contemplation must appear in some respects arbitrary. The more so if it includes, as this book does, peoples scattered all over the globe, with a great assortment of historical styles, and modes of subsistence that range from agriculture in a tropical forest to pastoralism in a near desert. Still the book has a rationale, and the peoples considered constitute a unity beyond the idiosyncratic compass of an author's personal knowledge. They represent a certain category of cultural development, intermediate in complexity between the mobile hunters and the gatherers and early agrarian states such as the Egyptian or Sumerian. They conjure up, then, a certain cultural era, that period, variable in its dimensions in different parts of the world, between the end of the Old Stone Age and the beginnings of civilization. *Tribesmen* is a study of the ethnographic heritage of Neolithic times. But above all, the peoples with which we deal are alike in cultural design. *Tribesmen* is a study of the primitive "segmentary societies."

The last point will require extended justification; here I offer merely a preliminary explanation. As I understand the term, "tribe" is like the "nation" of older usage, a body of people of common derivation and custom, in possession and control of their own extensive territory. But if in some degree socially articulated, a tribe is specifically unlike a modern nation in that its several communities are not united under a sovereign governing authority, nor are the boundaries of the whole thus clearly and politically determined. The tribe builds itself up from within, the smaller community segments joined in groups of higher order, yet just where it becomes greatest the structure becomes weakest: the tribe as such is the most tenuous of arrangements, without even a semblance of collective organization. The tribe is also uncomplicated in another way. Its economics, its politics, its religion are not conducted by different institutions specially designed for the purpose but coincidentally by the same kinship and local groups: the lineage and clan segments of the tribe, the households and villages, which thus appear as versatile organizations in charge of the entire social life. Such a cultural formation, at once structurally decentralized and functionally generalized, is a primitive segmentary society.

Emerging from Chapter 1, which is a discussion of "The Meaning of the Primitive" of a kind presently quite popular, the reader soon discovers that the unity of the book is the unity I allege of the societies considered: the segmentary tribal design. Chapter 2 attempts a general definition of that design; Chapter 3, the adaptational variations to which it is subject; Chapter 4, some main principles of social and political content; and Chapters 5 and 6, the way the tribal scheme orders economic and religious activities. I should say that the book was written for fledgling anthropologists and other interested spectators rather than for professional experts. A few sections nevertheless might cause technical difficulties, particularly those on cross-cousin marriage and Fijian kinship terminology in Chapter 4 (pp. 57–61 and 69–73). These I think could be lightly skimmed without losing the general train of argument.

A preliminary draft of this book was written while I was a fellow at The Center for Advanced Studies in the Behavioral Sciences in Palo Alto, California. I am grateful to The Center for the opportunity to indulge this and a hundred other whims. Gratitude also to Mervyn Meggitt, Roy Rappaport, and Eric Wolf for criticisms of the manuscript.

A book so largely about kinship ought to be dedicated to those who first taught me about it, patiently, with devotion and unending tolerance for a not always apt pupil: to my parents.

Marshall D. Sahlins

Contents

ix

One Tribesmen
in History and Anthropology

Not very long ago, there was a primitive world and a civilized world. On islands of the South Seas, in the jungles of South America and the grasslands of East Africa, tribal peoples were still constructing new versions of a kind of culture that in Europe was already a forgotten era. But to speak today of "the civilized world," implying some primitive outer darkness, is to speak the language of history. Modern civilization knows no borders: those curious peoples beyond the pale have been drawn into the main sphere in the course of Europe's four-century planetary reconnaisance. Once discovered, they were rapidly colonized, baptized, and culturally traumatized—"acculturated" is the technical term . . .

> Collapsed in equatorial acquiescence,
> Agreed to cultural obsolescence,
> Built dada villages of rusted scraps
> Of corrugated iron and busted water taps.

And now, having bit deeply into native custom, civilization allows itself the luxury of an intellectual digestion: the primitives are largely anthropologized.

(So anthropology, as one amateur practitioner cynically observed, becomes an inquest into the corpse of one society presided over by members of another.)

The Rise and Fall
of Tribal Culture

If the world today belongs to nation-states to do with what they will, in a similar way several thousand years ago it had fallen to tribal peoples. The spread of modern civilization has been likened to an evolutionary success story: the rise, extension, and diversification of an advanced type, spelling the displacement of primitive types. But the scenario had been produced before, on a prehistoric stage, during the transition from the Paleolithic to the Neolithic, with the advantage then going to tribal culture and displacement the fate of indigenous hunters and gatherers. On the momentum given by neolithic agriculture and animal husbandry, tribal peoples became dominant over much of the earth. The hunting life suddenly became a marginal strategy.

History had been decided by economic power. The same happens so regularly as to suggest the rule—or "law" as some are pleased to call it—that cultural dominance goes to technical predominance: the cultural type that develops more power and resources in a given environmental space will spread there at the expense of indigenous and competing cultures. This "Law of Cultural Dominance" explains in a general way the neolithic-tribal success story. Hunters and gatherers, unable to generate the manpower and organization to match intrusive neolithic régimes, could not hold the world's accessible and fertile environments against farmers and herders—unless the hunters themselves adopted domestication and transcended the paleolithic condition. In any event, once cultivation and husbandry appeared it was not long before roving food collectors were limited to inhospitable margins and interstices of a larger neolithic map. In isolated places, and in geographic extremes such as deserts where food collection yields higher returns than would neolithic techniques, the paleolithic might hold on. But now only as a historic sideshow.

All this had happened quickly—considering it from the total perspective of human history. The earliest farmers on archaeological record occupied hilly forests and valley oases of the Near East, where the Neolithic seems to have developed in the period 10,000 B.C. to 7000 B.C. By 2000 B.C. neolithic communities had been established the length of Eurasia, from Ireland to Indonesia. In the New World, food domestication began somewhat later than in the Old: the main staple of the American Neolithic, maize, seems to have been first brought under cultivation about 5000 B.C. in Middle America. After a period of slow gestation, neolithic culture spread widely and rapidly; by the time of Christ it was distributed from Peru to the American Southwest.

To this point, we have allowed ourselves some crude assumptions. Tribal peoples and cultures have been linked with neolithic techniques of production, as if the latter necessarily usher in evolutionary advances beyond the cultural capacities of hunters. One of the tasks of this book must be to refine such evolutionary equations and distinctions; or better, to make students knowledgeable enough to criticize them. Here then is one *caveat*: while it is true that most tribesmen are farmers or herders, thus cultural descendants of the Neolithic, not all are. Moreover, it is doubtful that tribal culture originated with the Neolithic Revolution; it could have emerged before. A complicated development of clans and chiefs, of a kind beyond the culture of mobile hunters and a kind we might like to call "tribal," occurred in recent times among Indians of America's Northwest Coast. The Kwakiutl, Nootka, Tsmishian, and other tribes of the American Northwest were as highly organized as most Indians north of Mexico. This is just to name one instance where *food collectors*, here blessed with abundant maritime resources, are known to have reached the cultural average of neolithic communities. So where nature is exceptionally prodigal, hunters and gatherers may surpass the cultural circumstances typical of that economic mode.[1] And the same could easily have happened during the later Paleolithic—here and there. The Neolithic, then, did not necessarily spawn tribal culture. What it did was provide the technology of tribal *dominance*.

Neolithic techniques equip societies to creatively transform their environments. Neolithic communities do not operate under the same natural constraints as hunters: food domestication allows agriculturists to maintain comparatively high degrees of cultural order in a variety of geographic settings; whereas hunters can do the same only where nature provides abundant wild food. Thus, while it is possible that a few favorably situated hunting societies of the Paleolithic advanced to tribal levels, a general advance of primitive culture on a planetary scale waited on the Neolithic Revolution. Likewise, most of the tribes with which we shall deal in this book are agriculturists and pastoralists, *food producers*, though some are hunters, fishers and gatherers.

The Neolithic was the historic day of tribesmen. But even as this day was dawning on the margins of Europe, Asia, and the Americas, the tribal sun was in eclipse in critical core areas. Civilization was coming into being, as early as 3500 B.C. in the Near East, and neolithic tribes were being superseded just as they had before superseded paleolithic hunters. By 2500 B.C. civilization had been developed in the Indus River Valley, by 1500 B.C. in the Yellow River Valley of China, by 500 B.C. in Middle America and Peru. This was a new dominant type, ever creating new varieties as it advanced, and ever opposing and undermining indigenous tribalism. Even before Europe began its self-appointed mission of giving "new worlds to the world," before, say, the sixteenth century, the distribution of tribal culture had been seriously curtailed. It was confined in the main to North America south of Canada and north of the Valley of Mexico, to the Caribbean and Amazonia, to portions of Africa south of the Sahara, to Inner Asia and Siberia, to the hinterlands of Southeast Asia, and to the islands of the Pacific Basin (Fig. 1.1).

These several areas make up the tribal world of modern cultural anthropology. Here we have not prehistory but *ethnography*—eyewitness accounts of tribes as going concerns. Indeed anthropologists, except as they become interested in recent cultural changes, rather like to think that the natives still exist in their pristine state—or at least talk about them that way. We adopt the convention of the "ethnological present," discussing the Iroquois or the

---

[1] See Elman R. Service's book in this Series, *The Hunters* (Englewood Cliffs, N.J.: Prentice-Hall, 1966).

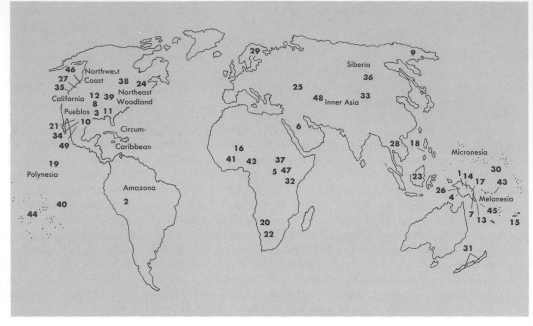

*Figure 1.1. Tribes and general culture areas noted in following chapters.
1. Abelam. 2. Amahuaca. 3. Arapaho. 4. Asmat. 5. Azande. 6. Beduoin.
7. Busama. 8. Cheyenne. 9. Chukchi. 10. Comanche. 11. Creek. 12. Crow.
13. Dobu. 14. Enga. 15. Fijians. 16. Fulani. 17. Gahuka-Gama. 18. Hanunóo. 19. Hawaiians. 20. Herero. 21. Hopi. 22. Hottentot. 23. Iban. 24.
Iroquois. 25. Kalmuk (Mongols). 26. Kapauku. 27. Kwakiutl. 28. Lamet.
29. Lapps. 30. Manus. 31. Maori. 32. Masai. 33. Mongols. 34. Navaho.
35. Nootka. 36. Northern Tungus. 37. Nuer. 38. Ojibway. 39. Sioux.
40. Tahitians. 41. Tallensi. 42. Tiv. 43. To'ambaita. 44. Tongans. 45.
Trobriands. 46. Tsimshian. 47. Turkana. 48. Turkic (Kazakh). 49. Zuni.*

Hawaiians as they were at the time of European discovery—that is, when they
were "really" Iroquois and Hawaiian. But of course there is more than anti-
quarian nostalgia in this convention: for comparative purposes it is necessary
to characterize primitive cultures apart from the distortions introduced by
Europeans. Indulge us, then, in this romantic manipulation of history, and
join in our contemplation of tribesmen—of the ethnological present.

Tribes and Civilizations:
The State of Nature and the Nature of the State

Hereby it is manifest, that during the time men live without a common
Power to keep them all in awe, they are in that condition which is called
Warre; and such a Warre, as is of every man, against every man.[2]

Tribes occupy a position in cultural evolution. They took over from simpler
hunters; they gave way to the more advanced cultures we call civilizations.
But civilization is not an advance over tribal society simply by reason of its
dominance-power. Civilization is an advance in organization, a qualitative
transformation of the culture type.

[2] Thomas Hobbes, *Leviathan*.

In its broadest terms the contrast between tribe and civilization is between War and Peace. A civilization is a society specially constituted to maintain "law and order"; the social complexity and cultural richness of civilizations depend on institutional guarantees of Peace. Lacking these institutional means and guarantees, tribesmen live in a condition of War, and War limits the scale, complexity, and all-round richness of their culture, and accounts for some of their more "curious" customs.

Obviously, I mean something different by "War" and "Peace" than is commonly understood. In fact, we ought to spell it "Warre" as Hobbes usually did, and with him intend by the word not just "battle" but a general disposition and right to fight, if necessary.

> For WARRE, consisteth not in Battell only, or the act of fighting; but in a tract of time, wherein the Will to contend by Battell is sufficiently known: and therefore the notion of *Time*, is to be considered in the nature of Warre, as it is in the nature of Weather . . . So the nature of War, consisteth not in actual fighting; but in the known disposition thereto, during all the time there is no assurance to the contrary. All other time is PEACE.[3]

In the social condition of Warre, force is a resort legitimately available to all men. There need not be violence, but neither is there assurance to the contrary. As a matter of fact, fighting may be at a discount within the tribe: a Hopi pueblo is as nonbelligerent a community as one may find. On the other hand, the everyday internal violence of the United States of America has few parallels in history or ethnography. But politically the American citizenry differ from the Hopi in this: they have "a common Power to keep them all in awe," a Government, which precludes that anyone take the law in his own hands, thus keeps the Peace. Tribes such as the Hopi lack a sovereign political and moral authority; the right to use force and do "battell," if not the inclination, is instead held by the people in severalty. Technically this is an internal social condition of Warre. Expressed another way, in the language of older philosophy, the U.S. is a state, the tribe a state of nature. Or, the U.S. is a *civilization*, the tribe a *primitive society*.

The state differentiates civilization from tribal society. The development of civilization was nothing less than a transformation in quality of the social system. A contrast with tribalism is not usefully made by reference to one or a few simple features. It has proved futile to search for some decisive invention standing at the evolutionary divide. Writing, for instance, does not make a civilization. Primitives are conventionally called "preliterate peoples," but lack of writing does not exclusively distinguish them, as the sophisticated yet illiterate native civilizations of Peru or West Africa will testify. Nor is urbanity in the literal sense of cities the litmus reaction of civilization. The appeal of such criteria of civilization as writing and cities is mainly to the preanthropological supposition that primitive peoples are essentially yokels.

Another conventional formula, "kinship to territory"—supposing primitive society to be "based on" kinship, civilization on territory—better expresses the evolutionary transformation. But it is overly compressed, and thereby vulnerable to naive criticism. The rankest anthropological novice can point

---

[3] *Ibid*.

out that many primitive peoples occupy and defend discrete territories; or that the constituent groups of tribal societies, such as lineages and clans, are often centered in territorial estates, and without its land the clan is dead. This criticism is informed enough of primitive society, but insufficiently informed of the meaning of "kinship to territory," which is a kind of evolutionary proverb, the metaphorical condensation of a complex development. At the least, "territory" should be here understood as a dominion, the realm of a sovereign power. The critical development was not the establishment of territoriality in society, but the establishment of society *as* a territory. The state and its subdivisions are organized as territories—territorial entities under public authorities—as opposed, for instance, to kinship entities under lineage chiefs. Sir Henry Sumner Maine, while arguing against the antiquity of territorial sovereignty in Europe, aptly epitomized its development out of tribal conceptions by certain changes in the title assumed by French kings: from the Merovingian "King of the Franks" to the Capetian "King of France."

A state has a true *government*, public and sovereign, structurally separated from the underlying population and set above them. The mass of people in the state domain become subjects, and the government sovereign, by virtue of the force vested in the latter. The right to control force has precipitated out of society at large to rest exclusively with government. No one in general has leave to proceed by force; only the government in particular has leave to decree the rules of social order and to enforce them—thus Peace is an internal condition of the system as constituted. More analytically, a state or civilized society is one in which: (1) there is an official public authority, a set of offices of the society at large conferring governance over the society at large; (2) "society at large," the domain of this governing authority, is territorially defined and subdivided; (3) the ruling authority monopolizes sovereignty—no other person or assembly can rightly command power (or force) except by sovereign delegation, leave, or consent; (4) all persons and groups within the territory are *as such*—by virtue of residence in the domain—subject to the sovereign, to its jurisdiction and coercion.

But "civilization," one might reasonably argue, has a much richer connotation. More than a formal political apparatus, it is a large and complex culture. The word conjures images of great cities and monumental architecture, dense populations and a wealth of goods. We think of a social system richly textured, with artisans and merchants, peasants, priests, proletarians and princes. Fair enough. But the objection may yet confirm our reasoning, the soundness of isolating the state as *the* criterion of civilization. A civilization is a society both massive and divided within itself. The population is large, perhaps ethnically diversified, divided by its labors into specialized occupations and, by unequal interests in the means of power, divided into unequally privileged classes. All the cultural achievements of civilization depend on this magnitude and complexity of organization. Yet a society so large, heterogeneous, and internally divided cannot stand without special means of control and integration. Consider the situation if everyone were left to protect and advance his own interests as best he could—if everyone might proclaim, *"l'état, c'est moi!"* The system would disintegrate in chaotic factionalism, sedition, and civil war. The cultural richness that we call civilization has to be instituted in state form.

Government is to the social organism as the central nervous system is to the biological organism. Just as in biological evolution, only a certain minimum of cultural complexity was possible prior to the development of a central, sovereign mechanism. That which "keeps them all in awe" keeps the differentiated parts of civilization in collaborative order—not, as I say, by abolishing violence but by making it illegitimate. To complete the analogy, a tribe is an animal without a central regulative system. Limits are thereby imposed on tribal scale, complexity, and overall cultural elaboration. Such are the disadvantages of Warre . . .

> Whatsoever therefore is consequent to a time of Warre, where every man is Enemy to every man; the same is consequent to the time, wherein men live without other security, than what their own strength, and their own invention shall furnish them withall. In such condition, there is no place for Industry; because the fruit thereof is uncertain: and consequently no Culture of the Earth, no Navigation, nor use of the commodities that may be imported by Sea; no commodious Building; no Instruments of moving, and removing such things as require much force; no Knowledge of the face of the Earth; no account of Time; no Arts; no Letters; no Society; and which is worst of all, continuall feare, and danger of violent death; And the life of man, solitary, poore, nasty, brutish, and short.[4]

We have learned much about primitive peoples since the seventeenth century. At this late date Hobbes reads like parody; his "nasty, brutish, and short" remark becomes now a favorite subject for textbook burlesque. But in thus congratulating ourselves at Hobbes' expense on matters about which we are better informed—thanks to the investigations of countless people over three centuries—we tend to overlook the things Hobbes knew better than we, and thus manage not to learn anything. The burden of the passage just cited is that where force is held in severalty, the society is inadequately organized to bear an elaborate cultural development. Here is a key to the comparative limitations of tribal society, and to the evolutionary significance of the State.

"The war of every man against every man" is also true—*although it has never happened*.[5] Individuals and subgroups of tribal society maintain the certain right and potential inclination to secure by force their safety, gain, and glory. In that event, Warre exists, but mainly in the form of an underlying circumstance. In *fact*, tribesmen live in kin groupings and communities within which feuding is usually suppressed, and they have benefit too of economic, ritual and social institutions conducive to good order. To speak of Warre, then, is to uncover by analysis tendencies ordinarily concealed by powerful impositions of the cultural system. Primitive anarchy is not the appearance of things. It is the unconscious of the system. Yet as the outward behavior of a person may not be intelligible except as the transfiguration of unconscious desires, so the objective organization of tribal society may only be understood as the repressive transformation of an underlying anarchy. Many of the special pat-

---

4 *Ibid.*

5 Hobbes neither insisted nor did he believe that Warre was ever a general empirical condition (see *Leviathan*, Part I, Chapter XIII).

One would, of course, part company with Hobbes on his apologia for absolutism, for which purpose his conception of the state of nature was a necessary condition. But we are not using the *Leviathan* as a political tract; for that we could have had Rousseau.

terns of tribal culture became meaningful precisely as defense mechanisms, as *negations of Warre*.[6]

For in a situation of Warre, where every man is empowered to proceed against every man, peacemaking cannot be an occasional inter-tribal event. It becomes a continuous process, going on within society itself. As much as Warre is implicit, that much does peacemaking become an explicit necessity . . .

> And because the condition of Man . . . is a condition of Warre of every one against every one; in which case every one is governed by his own Reason; and there is nothing he can make use of, that may not be a help unto him, in preserving his life against his enemyes; It followeth, that in such a condition, every man has a Right to every thing; even to one an-others body. And therefore, as long as this naturall Right of every man to every thing endureth, there can be no security to any man, (how strong or wise soever he be,) of living out the time, which Nature ordinarily alloweth men to live. And consequently it is a precept, or generall rule of Reason, *That every man, ought to endeavour Peace, as farre as he has hope of obtaining it; and when he cannot obtain it, that he may seek, and use, all helps, and advantages of Warre*. The first branch of which Rule, containith the first, and Fundamentall Law of Nature; which is, *to seek Peace, and follow it*.[7]

Man cannot in fact hope to survive unless Warre is regulated. Hobbes therefore held it a precept of reason that men seek Peace—and, further, that the play of reason could not be secured outside the state (Commonwealth). My point is that peacemaking is the wisdom of tribal institutions. Moreover, because tribal institutions must bear this political load, they are sometimes quite different from analogous institutions of civilizations. For in civilizations, Peace need not be built into, say, economic relations. Here law and order are secured by a specialized political organization, government, and imposed on the economy. So if a man charge "what the traffic will bear," the only licking he risks is the financial one.

Of course, not only tribes have had to control Warre. Hunters are at least as much in the state of nature and have been there much longer. Many of the peacemaking arrangements of tribal culture are similar to those of hunters and gatherers. Yet the potential of Warre is, if anything, increased by the advance to tribalism. Tribal techniques of production typically support more people, populations both more dense and more concentrated, than does simple hunting. The sheer number of Brownian contacts, hence of possible conflicts, increases. Uniquely valuable, stable and scarce resources are defined by tribal technologies: arable land, timber lots for forest agriculture, pasturage and water for cattle. Too, there are more goods in society—aside from new techniques of production, the immobility of tribal life makes feasible some accumulation of wealth—hence, more things to steal, loot or otherwise

---

[6] Perhaps this in turn accounts for the success of a certain kind of "functionalism" in anthropology: the explication of given social relations and customs by their contribution to "social solidarity" or "equilibrium." Primitive society is at war with Warre. Hence functionalism has unusual power and appeal as an anthropological theory.

[7] Hobbes, *Leviathan*.

quarrel over. Warre takes on new vistas among tribesmen. The tribal war on Warre is proportionately intense.

Take economic relations. Exchange in tribal societies generally proceeds under certain constraints. Competition and gain are often excluded, either in the attempt to make friendly relations or at least to avoid unfriendly ones.

In an uncommon number of tribal transactions material utility is played down, to the extent that the main advantages appear to be social, the gain coming in good relations rather than good things. I refer to the several varieties of "reciprocal gift-giving" (so-called), ranging from informal hospitality to the formal exchanges that seal a marriage or a blood brotherhood. These are *instrumental exchanges*; i.e., they establish solidarity between people through the instrumentality of things. (As we say—but on comparatively rare occasions—"it's the sentiment that counts.") In instrumental transactions, two parties may exchange goods with which both are already supplied. Sometimes—in establishing blood brotherhood, settling feud, or arranging marriage —the people give each other equal amounts of identical goods. A waste of time and effort? As the famous anthropologist Radcliffe-Brown observed of comparable dealings among Andamanese hunters: "The purpose . . . was a moral one. The object of the exchange was to produce a friendly feeling between the two persons concerned, and unless it did this it failed of its purpose." [8] Material benefit is not the issue, except it be the other party's benefit, for sacrifices may be made—in the interest of peace. The issue is peace.

And even where utilities are sought through exchange, due regard for the other person is usually politic. A transaction always has an instrumental coefficient: it is socially negative or positive, depending on how far material advantage is pressed or how much is given in return for favors received. An exchange is inevitably a social strategy. In Warre the strategic alternative is to be nice—or be prepared to fight. Therefore, *reciprocity*, or some approximation to it, dominates tribal economics. Reciprocity in exchange is economic diplomacy: the mutuality of the material flow symbolizes willingness to consider the other party's welfare, a disinclination to selfishly prosecute one's own. Here again Hobbes anticipates ethnography. In a time of Warre, he divined, reciprocity is a law of nature, consequent on the first law, which enjoins men to seek Peace:

> As Justice dependeth on Antecedent Covenant; so does GRATITUDE depend on Antecedent Grace; that is to say Antecedent Free-gift: and is the fourth Law of Nature; which may be conceived in this Forme, *That a man which receiveth Benefit from another of meer Grace, Endeavour that he which giveth it, have no reasonable cause to repent him of his good will.* For no man giveth, but with intention of Good to himselfe; because Gift is Voluntary; and of all Voluntary Acts, the Object is to every man his own Good; of which if men see they shall be frustrated, there will be no beginning of benevolence, or trust; nor consequently of mutuall help; nor of reconciliation of one man to another; and therefore they are to remain still in the condition of *War*; which is contrary to the first and Fundamentall Law of Nature, which commandeth men to *Seek Peace*.[9]

---

[8] A. R. Radcliffe-Brown, *The Andaman Islanders* (Glencoe, Ill.: The Free Press, 1948), p. 84.

[9] Hobbes, *Leviathan*.

Exchanges become peace treaties. The transactions show a willingness to live and let live. Marcel Mauss, in his well-known "Essay on the Gift," having recognized the Hobbesian circumstances, suggested there was little else for it— the people have to "come to terms":

> In these primitive and archaic societies there is no middle path. There is either complete trust or mistrust. One lays down one's arms, renounces magic and gives everything away, from casual hospitality to one's daughter or one's property. It is in such conditions that men, despite themselves, learnt to renounce what was theirs and made contracts to give and repay. But then they had no choice in the matter. When two groups of men meet they may move away or in case of mistrust or defiance they may resort to arms; or else they can come to terms.[10]

Nor are primitive peoples themselves unaware of the peace in their trade. In certain East African languages, "trade" or "barter" means also "peace." Perhaps this Bushman said it best:

> Demi said, "The worst thing is not giving presents. If people do not like each other but one gives a gift and the other must accept, this brings a peace between them. We give to one another always. We give what we have. This is the way we live together." [11]

Now take tribal social relations in general. They are, as the evolutionary proverb has it, dominated by kinship. Kinship is a social relation of cooperation and nonviolence (ordinarily). "Kindred" has the same root as "kindness," two words—as E. B. Tylor said—"whose common derivation expresses in the happiest way one of the main principles of social life." [12] Languages of tribesmen embody similar correspondences. Among the Nuer of East Africa, "kinship" is the word for "peace." In Fijian, the phrase *tiko vakaveiwekani*, "to be as (or live as) relatives" is applied to the establishment and condition of "living in peace." A Fijian term meaning "to be acquainted, to know one another" is the synonym of "to be related." On the other hand, "stranger" means also "not related" and for Fijians as for many other tribal peoples has a sinister connotation, if not the denotation of "enemy"—someone you can eat. Kinship is a fundamental ground of peaceful human discourse. The wide extension of kinship idioms, relations, and groups in tribal societies represents another way they seek peace.

This is not to claim that kinship prevails in tribal society just because of its political functions. The economic cooperation it sustains is equally vital and perhaps decisive. Also, I do not wish to claim that kinship is the sole tribal principle. Military, religious and age-grade associations not organized as kinship groups are widely distributed in Africa, Oceania, and aboriginal America. It

---

[10] Marcel Mauss, *The Gift* (London: Cohen and West, 1954), p. 79.

[11] Lorna Marshall, "Sharing, Talking, and Giving: Relief of Social Tensions Among Kung Bushmen," *Africa*, XXXI (1961), 245.

[12] Sir Edward B. Tylor, *Anthropology* (Ann Arbor: Ann Arbor Paperbacks, University of Michigan Press, 1960), p. 249.

might be observed, however, that these are often institutionally subordinate to the kinship design, that personal kinship with a member of the association is a common basis of recruitment, and that the idiom of group solidarity is frequently kinship—the associations are "brotherhoods." The last exemplifies the general propensity of tribal peoples to cloak alliances of convenience in kinship garb. Where peace is necessary or desirable, kinship is extended to effect it.

On the interpersonal level, kinship is widely extended through the tribe. Perhaps you are familiar with "classificatory kinship." It is characteristic of the very great majority of tribes. In classificatory schemes, certain people related to oneself in a direct line of descent are in a class with collateral relatives. Thus in a common classificatory usage, the brother of my father is related to me in the same way as my father: I call them both by the same term—translated, "father"—and behave more or less the same way toward both. Said differently, relatives of the same broad social status are classed together. My father and his brother may be in critical social attributes the same: males of my lineage of the same senior generation. The social similarity is embodied in a common kinship designation. Now, the important thing is that once kinship categories are thus widely defined they are widely extendable. If my father is socially equivalent to his brother, the latter's son is logically equivalent to my brother; hence FaBrSo=Br. By the same principles, my father's father and his brother are equivalent, my father's father's brother's son is "father," his son is "brother," and so on (Fig. 1.2). Classificatory kinship has a logic of expandability. However remote genealogically, kinsmen need not be lost track of, nor in fact conceived remote in kinship class. Of course the people can and do make distinctions between a mother's husband ("own" father) and other "fathers," and between "near" and "distant" kinsmen of a given class. But the expandability of kinship classes, and their manifest designation as familial categories, is an obvious help to peacemaking.

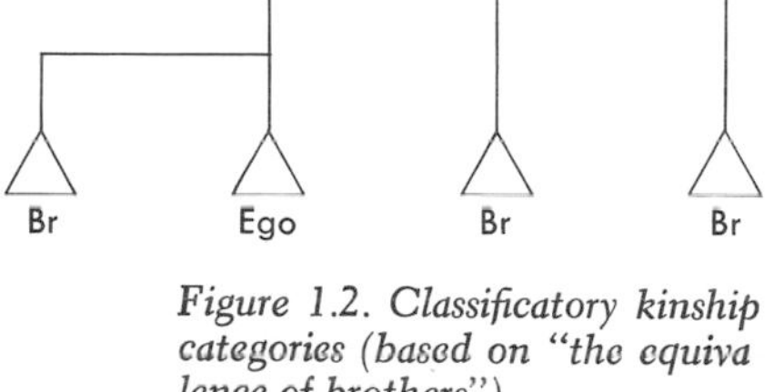

On the level of group organization, beyond the interpersonal level, tribes have made a main contribution to the repertoire of kinship. *Descent groups* are perhaps original with tribes: certainly not character-

Figure 1.2. *Classificatory kinship categories (based on "the equivalence of brothers").*

istic of hunters, yet run-of-the-mill in the tribal range. A descent group is a body of kinsmen united by common ancestry. Tribal descent groups vary extremely—e.g., in the mode of reckoning common descent, which may be through males only (*patrilineal*), females only (*matrilineal*), or males and females (*cognatic*). We are concerned at the moment with those that are *corporate*, in the sense of perpetual units of the tribal system, existing forever though individual members come and go through birth and death. The group has a destiny and a reality that transcend the mortal span of persons. It is a superperson, and its members are as one—so close perhaps as to be reckoned "brothers" and "sisters" if of the same generation, and perhaps forbidden to marry. Within such groups a Warre of *every* man against *every* man cannot materialize. To proceed by force against a fellow clansman is to proceed against oneself, which is contrary even to laws of nature, a sin, possibly subject to dire consequences of ancestral wrath. In some tribes the only safe conduct is in those places were clanship can be established; otherwise, except to make war people are well advised to stay home. In thus assuming protection of its members and precluding internal violence, descent groups push outward the sphere of Warre, at the minimum to some intergroup sector.

Yet even here diplomatic arrangements are possible. By further permutations of kinship principle, descent groups themselves can be allied by kinship. Intermarriage effects *alliance:* insofar as each group is a cohesive entity, marriages between members of different groups can be translated into marriages between the groups themselves. Kinsmen are made as well as born; they are made by marriages. And marriages are not made in heaven; they are made according to rules. A rule against marriage in one's own group enjoins marriage with another group. Beyond this, the rules may specify the kind of relatives whom one must or should marry; for example, someone related as "mother's brother's daughter." This sort of prescription, as we shall see, systematically relates lineages. Each such rule develops a determinate pattern of alliance between descent groups. Marital maneuvers are typically of consuming interest to tribesmen. For in the tribal war on Warre, marriage is an institutional strategy of first importance.

Now the lessons we have taken from tribal economics and kinship could also be drawn from other cultural sectors. Ritual in tribes (as in other types of culture) may be closely engaged in seeking peace. Confucius said: "Ceremonies are the bond that holds the multitudes together, and if the bond be removed, the multitudes fall into confusion." Public, communal rituals become fairly common at the tribal level. These rituals impose at the minimum a ceremonial peace, and by the implication of common dependence on supernatural powers instill a sense of the collectivity and of the *dependence* of every man upon every man. The latter effect may be heightened by a ceremonial division of labor among kin groups, each charged with a special ritual function or performance, such that collaboration becomes necessary to secure supernatural benefits. There are tribes—the Voltaic peoples of West Africa and the Pueblo Indians come to mind—where the burden of peacemaking rests most critically with ritual, as if in these densely populated yet socially fragmented communities the ordinary secular devices of good order must prove inadequate.

But enough said. The meaning is clear and needs no more repetition.

I have tried to show you that civilizations differ from tribes by virtue of their specialized political institutions, their governments, which sovereignly assume the power and right to protect the citizenry and maintain peace within the state. In tribal societies control of force is not withheld from the people; they are in that condition Hobbes called Warre, which is a fatal condition if not checked. Lacking *specialized* institutions of law and order, tribes must mobilize the generalized institutions they do have to meet the threat of Warre.

Economics, kinship, ritual, and the rest are so enlisted. In the process, by undertaking this political function, tribal institutions develop particular forms and particular expressions, different and curious perhaps, but each and all understandable as diplomatic arrangements for keeping a modicum of peace. Such is the wisdom of tribal institutions.

Two Tribal Culture
and Its Transformations

Different countries, different customs: no two tribes are the same in detail. Tribesmen, moreover, are like all people and any person: the more familiar with them one becomes the more difficult to recall one's first general impressions. So what I am about to do—which is to formulate a generalized design of tribal culture—is plainly hazardous and perhaps futile. But such is the magic of the sociologist's "ideal type" that, founded as it is on actual or pretended ignorance of the empirical diversity, inadequate as it is as a representation of complex realities, primitive as it may be as an intellectual procedure, it can yield remarkable insights into the particular case. I think the general model of tribal culture suggested here helps one understand particular tribes—at least a fair number of them.

The Tribal Design

According to classical social science text, all cultures are divisible into three parts: technology, social organization, and ideology. Of these components, technology is often conceived most fundamental and, with social relations of production, decisive for the system. The rest is "superstructure."

This scheme has been used with fair success to explain certain major developments in the evolution of culture, such as the great leap forward when agriculture was invented, or the broad advance set off by the Industrial Revolution. But as a statement of how tribes are organized and work, the scheme rather distorts things. For in tribes, production, polity, and piety are not as yet separately organized, and society not as yet a holy alliance of market, state and church. The tribal condition, as I said, is transcended the moment a state apparatus is differentiated from and imposed upon society at large. The tribal structure is generalized; in this lies its primitiveness. It lacks an independent economic sector or a separate religious organization, let alone a special political mechanism. In a tribe, these are not so much different institutions as they are different *functions* of the same institutions: different things a lineage, for instance, may do. Holding an estate in land, the lineage appears as an economic entity; feuding, it is a political group; sacrificing to the ancestors, a ritual congregation. "Economics" thus does not appear as a distinct component of the same order as "social organization," but as a certain deployment of generalized social groups and relations that also have other functions. Anthropological wisdom suggests we abandon the conventional analysis of culture into distinct economic, social-political, and ideological spheres, and begin instead with a general statement of the tribal social scheme.

The constituent units of tribal society on the ground make up a progressively inclusive series of groups, from the closely-knit household to the encompassing tribal whole. Smaller groups are combined into larger ones through several levels of incorporation. The particular arrangements vary, of course, but the scheme might read something like this: families are joined in local lineages, lineages in village communities, villages in regional confederacies, the latter making up the tribe or "people"—itself set in a wider, inter-tribal field. The smaller groups are usually cohesive kinship groups. The larger appear as social compacts of the smaller, integrated perhaps by personal kinship, clanship, or intermarriage. Ordinarily, the tribe as a whole is identified and distinguished from others by certain commonalities of custom and speech.

From one vantage, the perspective of an architectural elevation, the tribe presents itself as a pyramid of social groups, technically speaking as a "segmentary hierarchy" (Fig. 2.1a). The smallest units, such as households, are segments of more inclusive units, such as lineages, the lineages in turn segments of larger groups, and so on, like a pyramid of building blocks. We speak of a "segmentary system" not simply because it is built of compounded segments, but also because it is *only* so built: its coherence is not maintained from the above by public political institutions (as by a sovereign authority). The same tribal system, however, when viewed from any particular point within gives a different impression (Fig. 2.1b). From this vantage, the tribe is divided into concentric circles of kith and kin: the household in central position, a circle of lineage kinsmen surrounding it, a wider circle of village relations, on out to the tribal and inter-tribal spheres. Each sphere, otherwise a *level of organization,* becomes in this perspective a *sector of social relations,*[1] relations increasingly broad and dilute as one moves outward from the familial navel.

---

[1] One may speak equally here of "zones," "spheres" or "fields" of social relations. "Sector," indeed, is geometrically inappropriate, but it yields the only decent adjective, which is why I tend to prefer it.

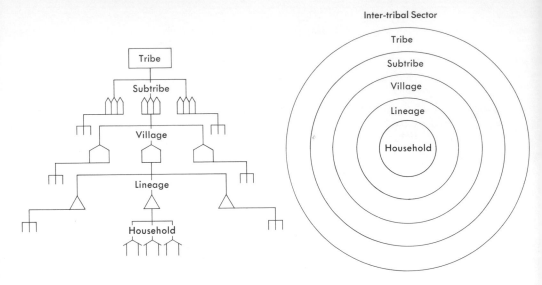

Figure 2.1. Generalized tribal design.

Now the strength of a tribe is generally in homestead and hamlet, the smallest groups and narrowest spheres. Here, at the tribal infrastructure, social interaction is greatest and cooperation most intense. This cohesion expresses in a general way the limitations of neolithic or advanced hunting economies: small-scale production, restricted division of labor, underdeveloped transport and communication, and comparatively low productivity. The social system, accordingly, becomes weaker where it is greater: the degree of integration decreases as the level of organization increases, and degrees of sociability diminish as fields of social relation broaden. The tribe (as a whole) is often the weakest link in the segmentary chain. Its peripheral communities develop close relations and cultural similarities with neighboring peoples, setting in motion a marginal erosion of tribal integrity, and rather than a definite inter-tribal border one comes upon an ambiguous zone of transition. Rarely united politically, often not definable with precision, the "tribe" may be beset by a crisis of identity: it is nameless, except as the people are considered "Stinkers" or something to that effect by their neighbors.

The model before us is set out in social terms. But more than a scheme of social relations, it is an organization of culture. The several levels of organization are, in the jargon of the trade, *levels of sociocultural integration*; the sectors, *sectors of sociocultural relations*. That is to say, first, that each level (each kind of group) has a range of functions: economic, ceremonial, defensive, and so forth—each organizes certain necessary tasks. Moreover, each sector as a more or less solidary field of co-membership has its values and morality, which govern the conduct of human affairs within that field. The terms of economic exchange, the weapons of political dispute—in short, the conditions of any cultural transaction—vary according to the sectoral distance of the parties. Functions are regulated by levels of organization, and transactions by sectors of relation.

A vintage joke has it that in the average American family the wife decides the little things, like whether to buy a new home, while her husband takes care of major problems—should we or should we not invade China, for

example. Something of the same division of labor applies in the tribal segmentary system: workaday problems fall mainly to smaller groups, while
major issues are resolved by the higher organization. The family, with its
domestic division of labor by sex and age, is constituted for day to day production—both of subsistence goods and many handicrafts—and neighbors of the
home community can usually be relied on for further assistance. Thus, not only
production but the circulation of goods (as domestic pooling and mutual aid)
is most intense at homebred levels of society. The smaller groups too take
possession of, or enjoy direct access to, strategic property, the resources and
technical means of production. But the functions of domestic groups are more
than economic—and also go beyond the care, education, and socialization of
the young. The household is a political entity, and in a tribal society, one of
some consequence. A little chiefdom within the chiefdom, it is mainly self-
regulating, as it is self-organized by the niceties of respect and authority embodied in familial relations. Indeed, a father usually has greater power to keep
his house in order than has any community leader in his domain: at least a
man can take a stick to his own child (and perhaps his wife), but the village
tyrant who lives by the club risks dying by it. Moreover, "the family that
prays together. . . ." Religion too has a lower-level existence, a substratum
concerned with personal well-being, which may bring together social intimates
to placate the spirits of illness or other misfortune; not to mention ceremonies
for the benefit of the household or the lineage as a group, agricultural rituals
for instance, that invoke such socially appropriate supernatural parties as
family ghosts and lineage ancestors. The tribal infrastructure has a great
range of local meanings and purposes.

More general difficulties are confronted by greater communities. Some
things, like rain, epidemic, or crop failure, happen to everyone. "Everyone"
then—that is, the village or all the villages thereabouts—may combine in
supplication of the great supernatural agencies governing the common fate.
It hardly needs saying that the feelings of collectivity and interdependence
thus inspired help strengthen these larger groups. The way may be paved for
cooperation in secular affairs, say communal construction of technical facilities,
regional trade, or aid to neighboring communities suffering food shortages.
The regional economy, however, is usually episodic, if it emerges at all. The
tribal superstructure is a political arrangement, a pattern of alliances and
enmities, its design shaped by tactical considerations. Overarching relations of
clanship or regional confederacy seem most often compelled by competitive
threats, in connection with which large-scale economic and ritual cooperation
may play the derivative role of underwriting cohesion in the face of external
dangers. The formation of regional polities, however, is frequently difficult for
tribesmen—for some of the same reasons that would make it useful. Higher
unity has to contend with the segmentary divisions of the infrastructure, with
economically self-centered local groups prepared to define and defend their
own interests against all comers. This anarchy may prove a serious liability,
perhaps too deeply instituted to overcome.

Western culture, with its differentiations of kinship, politics, religion, and
economics, does not properly equip us to understand a tribal segmentary order.
When we think of "religion" we already have in mind some (fairly) consistent set of beliefs, practices, and organization, systematic and self-contained,

distinctive and set apart from other "things in life"—something done on Sunday, and undone the rest of the week. This may be inappropriate in a tribal context, as it is inappropriate to speak of *the* religion of a tribe. The tribal religion is organized at various segmentary levels. To appreciate the "system" in it, religious practice has to be dissected into its component levels and related to the social constitution and life problems of the groups at issue. Perhaps only then does one discover, or begin to understand, the pattern of order in a seeming bewildering array of spiritual entities. The spirits have their own hierarchy, often recognized as such by the people: here is a substratum of animistic souls, then an intermediate level of ancestral beings, and above everything a supernatural upper class of great nature gods. The "system" is the segmentary system of the tribe, the ranking of the spirits a symbolic transposition of the segmentary hierarchy. The high gods are tribal gods, spirits of everyone, concerned with things that happen to everyone. Ancestral spirits are tutelaries of the clan or lineage, concerned with the particular destinies of these groups; while ghosts of the recently departed, forest sprites, or it may be the magical power of "medicines," particularly influence familial and individual fate. Of course, it may be possible to appeal to higher powers from lower quarters, but different classes of spirit have as their primary congregations social groupings of different order. And if the people say, on one hand, that the souls of the dead hover about their former houses as malevolent ghosts, and on the other hand that the dead travel to an ancestral other-world from which they benevolently watch over the living, one need not come to dim conclusions about the people's mental capacities—or even, to the conclusion that they believe every person to have two souls. The seemingly contradictory beliefs belong to different social contexts, and by that token are not brought into confrontation. The consistency of belief here is not internal, but in its relation to the social order: its organization by levels of sociocultural integration.

This will afford some idea of the virtues of conceiving the tribal segmentary system in its hierarchical dimension. Other understandings are gained by taking it from the perspective of expanding sociocultural spheres.

The several sectors of a tribe are graded by sociability. High and positive in the inner sphere of close kinship, sociability declines as the sector of social relations expands, becoming increasingly neutral in distant circles and ultimately, in the inter-tribal field, altogether negative. Now a transaction between any two parties—it may be economic, political, or of other content—places itself in some sector of tribal community: it engages the narrowest sector of co-membership of the parties. It is a lineage relation, or a transaction between co-villagers, or between fellow tribesmen. Each such sector, moreover, prescribes a standard of conduct: the transaction falls under an existing body of use and wont, as is consistent with the degree of common interest. Thus the sectoral scheme orders various dealings between people.

The rule is subject to certain exceptions, however, because kinship and clanship may be widely established, involving people in special relationships outside their own village or district. Not all a man's close kinsmen live in the neighborhood. And clansmen, though perhaps men living far down the river whom one has never met before, have to be treated with consideration: they are brothers and not strangers. Still, it is broadly true that close kinsmen reside nearby and distant kin far away—if only because kinsmen living nearby are close in a sociological sense and kinsmen who live at a distance are distant kinsmen. And as the quality of kinship is thus depreciated by social distance, the quality of mercy is strained. Consider how this affects terms of economic exchange in a Solomon Islands tribe:

> Mankind [to the Siuai people] consists of relatives and strangers. Relatives are usually interlinked by both blood and marital ties; most of them live nearby, and persons who live nearby are all relatives. . . . Transactions among them should be carried out in a spirit devoid of commerciality—preferably consisting of sharing, non-reciprocable giving, and bequeathing, among closest relatives, or of lending among more distantly related ones. . . . Except for a few very distantly related sib-mates [i.e., clansmen], persons who live far away are not relatives and can only be enemies. Most of their customs are unsuitable for the Siuai, but a few of their goods and techniques are desirable. One interacts with them only to buy and sell—utilizing hard bargaining and deceit to make as much profit from such transactions as possible.[2]

Political behavior is similarly qualified. Weapons of dispute commonly have a segmentary calculus, nicely graded in deadliness in a progression with sectoral distance. Matters should not go beyond heated words in family arguments, and though fists may fly in village brawls and spears be raised in intervillage feuds, the fatal poisoned arrow is reserved for tribal enemies. Conversely, the compulsion to negotiate is greater where the social sector of the argument is narrower. Within the home community, not to mention the family, conflict must be speedily suppressed on pain of breaking the group apart. Within the tribe, feuds ought to be settled and injury compounded—sooner or later. But enmity toward other tribes may be eternal.

In its broadest meaning, this sectoral design is a moral plan of the tribal universe. Hence its influence on economic and political conduct, which are different forms of moral conduct. The morality involved is principally kinship morality. It is grounded on considerations of sameness (of the same kind, kindness, kindred) and common interest, of which the customary idiom is familistic. The concentric social fields are so many steps of diminishing oneness, thus so many moral distinctions in "the way it's done."

But then, a contrast between tribal and civilized moral orders is suggested —between relative and situational norms as opposed to universal imperatives. In the tribal framework, a given act is not in itself good or bad whomever it may concern; it depends on exactly whom it does concern. Stealing another man's goods or his woman is a crime in one's own community, but the same act if perpetrated against an outsider can be a deed of merit. The suggested contrast with the absolute injunctions of modern law and ethics may be overdrawn.[3] No moral scheme is strictly absolute—especially in a time of war, when thou *shalt* kill some people—and maybe none is strictly contextual.

---

[2] Douglas Oliver, *A Solomon Islands Society* (Cambridge: Harvard University Press, 1955), pp. 454–455.

[3] Ancient law, however, might stipulate different punishments (implying different degrees of injustice) for a given wrong, depending on the class standings of the offender and injured party, as in the Hammurabi Code.

Still, universalist injunctions are singularly required in state (civilized) societies confronting the emergent problem of keeping the peace of a heterogeneous domain within which conflict of interest is a condition of organization.
In tribal circumstances, free reign is given to homebred ideas of right and
wrong—and charity begins at home. A sectoral morality thus prevails among
tribesmen, and in sufficient contrast to ourselves to draw repeated ethnographic comment. For example:

> Navaho morality is . . . contextual rather than absolute. . . . Lying is not
> always and everywhere wrong. The rules vary with the situation. To de-
> ceive when trading with foreign tribes is a morally accepted practice. Acts
> are not in themselves good or bad. Incest [by definition, a contextual sin]
> is perhaps the only conduct that is condemned without qualification. It is
> quite correct to use witchcraft techniques in trading with foreign tribes.
> . . . There is an almost complete absence of abstract ideals. Under the
> circumstances of aboriginal life Navahos did not need to orient themselves
> in terms of abstract morality. . . . In a large, complex society like modern
> America, where people come and go and business and other dealings must
> be carried on by people who never see each other, it is functionally neces-
> sary to have abstract standards that transcend an immediate concrete
> situation in which two or more persons are interacting.[4]

Segmentary Tribes and Chiefdoms

Our tribal design is so far just a bare outline. Initially it had to be
stated that way, to enjoy the pretense of covering the wide differences among
tribes of the real world. Now we must begin to inform ourselves of these
differences and accordingly inform the general model, incorporating into it
more detail and indicating the transformations to which it is subject.

Tribes present a notable range of evolutionary developments—taking "evolution" in its aspect of all-around cultural advance—which counterpose at
the extremes two radically different types. At the underdeveloped end of the
spectrum, barely constituting an advance over hunters, stand tribes socially
and politically fragmented and in their economies undiversified and modestly
endowed. These are *segmentary tribes* proper. But in its most developed expression, the *chiefdom*, tribal culture anticipates statehood in its complexities.
Here are regional political regimes organized under powerful chiefs and
primitive nobilities, often encompassing diversified as well as productive
economies. The segmentary tribe is a permutation of the general model in
the direction of extreme decentralization, to the extent that the burden of
culture is carried in small, local, autonomous groups while higher levels of
organization develop little coherence, poor definition, and minimum function.
The chiefdom is a development in the other direction, toward integration of
the segmentary system at higher levels. A political superstructure is established, and on that basis a wider and more elaborate organization of economy,
ceremony, ideology, and other aspects of culture.

---

[4] Clyde Kluckhohn, "The Philosophy of the Navaho Indians," in Morton H. Fried, ed.,
Readings in Anthropology (New York: Crowell, 1959), Vol. II, p. 434.

Between the most advanced chiefdom and the simplest segmentary tribe stand many intermediate arrangements. We shall concentrate on the widest contrasts; it will give some idea of the range of development among tribesmen.

The segmentary tribe is the main type in Amazonia, aboriginal California, Melanesia, northeastern North America, and several parts of Africa. American Indians of the Great Plains, the Northwest Coast, and the Pueblos of the Southwest are advanced in certain respects, but fall generally in the same class.

The segmentary tribe is sharply divided into independent local communities ("primary political segments"). These communities are small. They rarely include more than few hundred people, usually many less, and except among hunters and pastoralists rarely claim more than a few square miles as their own domain. In form of settlement the primary segment may be a compact village or an "open community" of scattered homesteads or hamlets. The precise organization also varies: in some tribes the autonomous community is a single descent group (e.g., a lineage), in others an association of several different lineages, in still others a loose network of kith and kin that ultimately entangles everyone (a local kindred). But whatever the precise organization, it will be the same as other communities of the tribe: the several primary segments are "structually equivalent." And each does for itself, economically and in other ways, what the others do for themselves: they are also "functionally equivalent."

These communities too are politically equal. By some good fortune, one may exceed another in prowess; yet none is by right superior and none by structure subordinate, but all are as good in the sight of men—if not, by their own lights, more so—and apt to proclaim the fact at the slightest provocation. Jealous of their own sovereignty, they recognize no greater political cause standing over and against their separate interests. Certain groups may ally for a time and a purpose, as for a military venture, but the collective spirit is episodic. When the objective for which it was called into being is accomplished, the alliance lapses and the tribe returns to its normal state of disunity.

As is the political scheme generally, leadership in segmentary tribes is confined in scope, mainly to the primary community—and often it is not even that extensive. One discerns two distinct sociological types among these local authorities, *petty chieftains* and *big-men*, sometimes both in the same tribe.

A petty chieftain is a "duly constituted authority," the official headman of a community or local descent group. The distinguishing feature of petty chieftainship, apart from its pettiness, is its officialness. That is to say, it is an office position: the chief does not make his pre-eminence so much as come into it, and his followers are not so much personal subordinates as they are subject to the office as members of the group. Succession to the headship may pass by descent; or it may fall by custom to the oldest man. In either event, the distinction gained is slight—the absence of a formal title beyond some such appellation as "the old man" is characteristic, and symptomatic of the underdevelopment of official authority. The chieftain is usually spokesman of his group and master of its ceremonies, with otherwise little influence, few functions, and no privileges. One word from him and everyone does as he pleases. But then, things usually manage to take care of themselves in communities of close kinsmen who know how to do right by each other and are usually so inclined—on pain of ridicule and a breakdown of reciprocity.

As a generic class of leadership, official chieftainship has a great career ahead of it, but at the stage of the segmentary tribe it must yield prominence to the more spectacular "big-man." Here is a man who does not come into an existing position of leadership over a certain group but personally acquires dominance over certain other fellows, a man who rises above the common herd—and indeed among certain cattle-keeping peoples is styled "the bull"—who makes himself a leader by making others followers: a fisher of men, inducing compliance by the strength of his personality, by his persuasiveness, perhaps by his prowess as a warrior, magician, or gardener, and often by calculated disposition of his wealth, which puts people under obligation to him and constrains their circumspection. This is a prince among men: men heed him because he is princely. He is not a Prince of Danes—whom men would heed if they were Danes. Though he holds no office or ascribed power, he does hold a grip on others and a superior reputation—by consensus he is, in the Melanesian phrase, a "big-man." Just how much influence such a paragon will command seems to depend on the structure of the tribe and the involvement of the local community in various maneuvers of cooperation and competition with other groups. Critical external dealings, political and economic, may be left to big-men—simply by the absence of compelling superstructural arrangements, such as lineage relations between different settlements. The welfare of his community hinges in that case on the big-man's arrangements, and his influence within the group is accordingly augmented. Representing their followers to the world at large, big-men of certain Melanesian tribes move from strength to strength. Gaining renown among other local groups, a big-man may succeed in uniting them all for war, ceremony, or trade. But this greater union is usually temporary, and so also the leader's greater sway. For the most part he remains a big-man in a little pond, and that only as long as he remains an impressive character.

The economy of the segmentary tribe is as atomistic as the political system. Production is generally small-scale, with enough manpower available in the village, not to say the family, for main tasks of livelihood. Besides, as each community produces much the same things, none is substantially dependent on another for specialized products. The tribal economy is not integrated by a localized division of labor and the exchange of complementary goods.

The relation of the primary segment to the tribal landscape proclaims its independence. The community's domain lies across the grain of natural resources, incorporating the range of environments to which the tribal technology is customarily adapted. The minimal political group holds farming land of different types, pasturage, hunting territory—whatever is deemed necessary for a human (tribal) existence. The local economy is the tribal economy in miniature. Each group, exploiting like environmental opportunities, underwrites, by its ecological completeness, its political autonomy.

It is possible that tribal settlements at a distance, situated in somewhat different environments, will diverge in production and set up a moderate trade. Even where local environments are similar they may be differentially fertile, and certain groups, subjected to seasonal food shortages, are forced to apply to fellow tribesmen for relief. Yet it is perhaps more common for tribesmen to develop regular trade with outsiders than with each other. For neighboring tribes often set their border along some ecological seam—a line between coast and hinterland, upland and valley, forest and plain—and establish within their respective zones unique patterns of adaptation. As producers of complementary goods, settlements of different tribes may then enter into strategic exchange: a crucial flow of materials penetrates the cultural boundaries. Prehistorians have argued that the "typical neolithic community" was self-sufficient. Yet the evidence of ethnography and archaeology suggests that inter-tribal division of labor and trade are commonplace, possibly because the adaptations of the simpler tribes tend to be narrow and ecologically specific.

Within a tribe, nevertheless, exchange may be socially enjoined even if ecologically unnecessary. For goods pass between the communities in instrumental transactions, such as marriage payments and blood compensations, in the interests of peace and alliance. It seems remarkable that these goods should be exotic items procured in trade with foreigners. Instrumental social payments are often the main means for distribution within the tribe of goods obtained from outside. But then, foreign items can contribute singularly to internal peacemaking. People are satisfied to be friends because that way they acquire things otherwise not available: the payment is a rare gift, socially effective on the principle of "it's just what I needed."

It is well that something "tribal" finally emerges in this discussion, for the emphasis on segmentary cleavages in economy and politics threatens to condemn tribalism to an analytic death (exactly the sentence some anthropological theoreticians would pass on it). In the background tribalism fairly belongs, but it is there, and its disturbing presence insists on some accounting for it. Perhaps most critical in giving a tribal people that measure of coherence and identity they do possess is their cultural similarity. The local groups are like each other in custom and speech, even as they often differ in these respects from others. Cut from the same cloth, they have a common destiny or, more technically, a "mechanical solidarity." Insofar as these groups are alike, they respond the same way to the world and thus develop an historic identity if not exactly a polity. Also important is the social nexus linking neighboring settlements of a tribe. The primary community is rarely endogamous. Marriages bridge political divisions, as do the ties of kinship issuing from these marriages. Then, there are certain *pan-tribal institutions*, widespread tribal associations: not exactly "groups" since they do not act as collectivities, but more like fraternal orders with chapters established in different locales—so that for the price of a secret handshake one may be able to cadge a free lunch in another place. The *clan* is a typical institution of this type: a multilocal, patrilineal or matrilineal descent unit—often widely dispersed in local lineages—the members of which do not intermarry because of their presumed common ancestry, but by that token stand ready to help each other if called upon. Since people have to marry outside the clan, into other clans, the tribe takes shape as a number of interconnected clans cutting across the several local groups. A set of age-grades or of religious or military societies may in an analogous way tie together tribal political segments. Still, tribal feelings and intercommunity connections are not always to be trusted in a showdown—Melanesian villages have been known to ally with foreign trade-partners in wars against communities of their own kind—testimony to the spirit of tribalism!

Thus the segmentary tribe.

The chiefdom overcomes its limitations, transcending its segmentary distinctions by an administrative hierarchy that reduces the local community to the status of a political subdivision. Chiefdoms are best exemplified in the island societies of Polynesia and Micronesia, in Circum-Caribbean America, among nomads of Central Asia, and among the Southwest African Bantu.

A chiefdom is a ranked society. The descent and community groups of a segmentary tribe are equal in principal, but those of a chiefdom are hierarchically arranged, the uppermost officially superior in authority and entitled to a show of deference from the rest. A chiefdom is not a class society. Although a stage beyond primitive equalitarianism, it is not divided into a ruling stratum in command of the strategic means of production or political coercion and a disenfranchised underclass. It is a structure of degrees of interest rather than conflicts of interest: of graded familial priorities in the control of wealth and force, in claims to others' services, in access to divine power, and in material styles of life—such that, if all the people are kinsmen and members of society, still some are more members than others. For some are of superior descent. Yet, where rank is thus linked to descent, status positions are often so subtly differentiated that no one can say, or will admit, where "chiefliness" leaves off and "commonality" begins. "Commoners" are usually kinsmen of "nobles," and the indigenous terms are applied relatively: a man who is a "commoner" in reference to some high chief is yet "noble" in relation to those kinsmen he outranks—though they may be merely his own children and the context of discussion is but his own household.[5]

One particular type of chiefdom organization, developed on exactly such distinctions of kinship grade, is so often called to anthropological mind it has come to epitomize the class. This is the Polynesian type, based on the *conical clan*. The conical clan system is not in fact confined to Polynesia: it is widespread in Central Asia and parts of Africa; and it may have had a role in the making of Western society, as it appears to have been the historic order of the Celtic peoples—e.g., the Scottish clan—and perhaps also the Biblical Israelites.

The conical clan is an extensive common descent group, ranked and segmented along genealogical lines and patrilineal in ideological bias (Fig. 2.2). Here is clanship made political. Distinctions are drawn between members of the group according to genealogical distance from the ancestor: the first-born son of first-born sons ranks highest and other people lower in the measure of their descent, down to the last born of last-born sons—everyone's commoner. A rule of primogeniture is implied: the oldest son should succeed to his father's authority. A second implication is that any group of descendants from a common ancestor will be divided into a senior branch (main line) and ranked junior branches (cadet lines). These principles apply throughout the structure: among the children of any house, the houses of any lineage, and the lineages of any inclusive lineage on up to the clan as a whole. Now the chiefdom as a political unit is constructed on the clan as a ranked descent unit.

---

[5] Thus an ethnographer of long experience among the Maori of New Zealand wrote of them: "Inasmuch as all members of a tribe are connected with well-born families, then it becomes a difficult matter to define the *ware* or *tutua* class, the people of low degree. Never have I met a native who would admit he was a member of that class." Elsdon Best, *The Maori*, Memoirs of the Polynesian Society, No. 5 (Wellington, 1924), Vol. 1, p. 346.

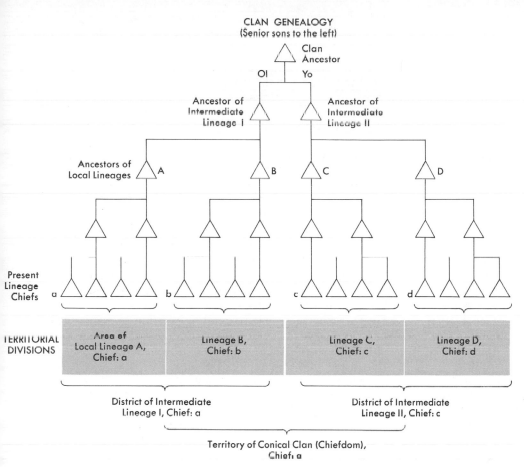

Figure 2.2. *Schematic model of chiefdom integrated on conical clan lines.*

In an ideal way, leaving aside various complications reality may introduce, Fig. 2.2 illustrates the integration of a chiefdom on conical clan lines. Small lineage sections (*Lineages A, B, C,* and *D*) comprise or dominate local settlements and supply from their senior house local chieftains. The leading local lineages of a given district are related as "brothers"—i.e., as descendants of brothers—and so make up a higher-order lineage (e.g., *Lineage I*) dominant in the district. The chieftain descended in the main line of this lineage (*Chief: a*) is the paramount chief of the district. In the same way, at the highest level, the conical clan provides the structure for the chiefdom as a whole: the paramount of the chiefdom is the direct descendant of the clan-ancestor— and the latter is exalted in status to the major deity of the political group. It may be that the tribe as such is constituted as a single clan-chiefdom, but more often it is divided into several independent chiefdoms, fighting over who is finest in the jungle.

Political organization is thus established above and beyond the community level. Political economy develops in proportion. Workaday production is still centered in the homesteads and villages, but masses of people may be called out for the building of an extensive irrigation complex, a great temple, or the stylish home of the paramount. On a ruling chief's command, goods and services are levied against the people for these enterprises, or for support of the chief and his retinue of ceremonial and executive officials, noble relatives, and idle hangers-on. But the chiefdom not only goes beyond the local economy, it breaks into the local economy and eggs it on. Chiefly pressure, political pressure, intensifies household production beyond household needs, and diverts the excess ("surplus") into the collective economy.

The chiefdom economy usually develops as well in another way, toward more diversification. A greater specialization of labor is evolved on an enlarged subsistence base. And by comparison with segmentary tribes, the subsistence sector itself may be more varied. It remains true of chiefdoms, as of the segmentary tribes, that the independent political group is set across the ecological grain, incorporating the range of landscapes normally encountered in the general area. But the scale of things can make a difference. Spread over a hundred square miles, a chiefdom is likely to encompass greater environmental variety than is included in the few square miles of a village domain. Moreover, a chiefdom has the means to organize, or at least tolerate, localized adaptations to the medley of its environmental opportunities. Chiefdoms have been known to combine several specialized local economies, involving different types of agriculture and agricultural staple, or some mixture of agriculture, herding, fishing, and perhaps trading. The economy is comparatively organic. Indeed, the division of labor *within* a chiefdom may be as great as that *between* adjacent segmentary tribes. Where in Melanesia a line between coastal fishers and inland taro gardeners is almost always a cultural divide, in Hawaii both patterns and others besides were incorporated in the same organization. This is a classic kind of evolutionary progress—the ability to organize greater economic and environmental diversity within a single cultural scheme, indeed, within a single political group.

To this advance the development of chieftainship itself is essential. In the chiefdoms, official authority surpasses by far its petty antecedents in the segmentary tribes. To speak of the greater social scope and power of paramount chiefs does not completely document the advance. What has been wrought is not just greater chiefs but a *system* of chieftainship, a hierarchy of major and minor authorities holding forth over major and minor subdivisions of the tribe: a chain of command linking paramount to middle-range and local-level leaders, and binding the hinterland hamlet to the strategic heights. The petty chieftain of the segmentary tribe is by comparison an inconspicuous figure in what social anthropologists call an "acephelous society."

In the chiefdoms, this extensive organization is combined, moreover, with the advantages of office power. Chiefdom leaders hold official positions with built-in privileges (as well as obligations) in regard to definite groups. Where a big-man is forced to engage in every variety of artful maneuver to accumulate wealth, and then tactfully distribute it to engender personal loyalties and more wealth, the chief has as a matter of noble due a lien on the allegiance, and the goods, of his people. A chief is a true authority: his is the power of the group rather than the person, given by the structural obligations of others to honor and obey him. Perhaps then he waxes fat and just *is* a big man—thus evoking the classic response of the Polynesian informant to what he had to consider the anthropologist's naiveté: "Can't you see he's a chief. See how big he is!" [6] But the big chief's own largeness is not the most significant of his sociological accomplishments; at the same time, he enlarges economic, political, and ceremonial life beyond the parochial conceptions of segmentary tribes.

Thus the chiefdom is united where the segmentary tribe is divided, and culturally integrated at higher levels, where the segmentary tribe is poorly defined. Again, the student must realize that these are but polar permutations of the tribal design, that the real world introduces many intermediate versions. The position of a given tribe along this continuum may be understood, at least in part, from the way it is related to nature and to coexisting societies, its mode of adaptation. The next chapter is about that.

---

[6] Edward Winslow Gifford, *Tongan Society*, Bernice P. Bishop Museum Bulletin No. 61 (Honolulu: Bishop Museum Press, 1929), 124.

Three Tribal
Adaptations

The early neolithic communities of the Near East had "mixed economies," combining animal husbandry (cattle, sheep, goat and pig) with grain cultivation (wheat and barley). But as the "neolithic revolution" spread from these and other centers, specialized modes of livelihood developed out of the generalized prototypes. New environments were encountered, different peoples began to participate in the "revolution," and unique experiments in domestication were attempted with local plants and animals. Neolithic culture traveled and in the process diversified. It underwent an *adaptive radiation*.

Arriving late on the scene, the anthropologist discovers not one tribal life-style but a whole array of them. Some tribesmen are indeed hunters and gatherers: by creative adaptations of paleolithic technique in areas marginal to advanced economies they managed to survive till an ethnographer could get a look at them. Other tribesmen, the majority, represent diverse end-products of the neolithic radiation. Each tribe thus appears as a special ecological type: each has its own life problems—its own environmental circumstances—and each has constructed an appropriate response.

Of course, there are as many adaptive variations as there are tribes. Again we have an embarrassment of empirical riches. But on broad definitions it is possible to block out some widely distributed and contrastive *ecotypes*. And it

28

is possible to say, also in a broad way, how these adaptations carry into tribal structure itself, generating certain permutations of the general model with which we have been working.[1]

Forest Agricultural Tribes

A specific form of neolithic production is characteristically practiced in tropical forests. Distinguished by skillful techniques of "slash-and-burn cultivation," it is ordinarily biased on the agricultural side, coupled perhaps with some food collecting and perhaps some reliance on domestic animals. This adaptation was once familiar in the New World as well as the Old, and in temperate as well as tropical forest—in Africa a "hoe-and-burn" variant also developed in scrub and grassland. In recent millennia, more intensive agricultural systems have taken over the temperate zones, so that slash-and-burn is now preeminently a tropical technique. Nevertheless, according to a recent U.N. report,[2] some 14 million square miles—inhabited by 200 million people—are still farmed by these time-tested methods. This is not all tribal domain: slash and burn is found as well in peasant hinterlands of sophisticated civilizations. Forest agricultural tribes, however, are notably represented; e.g., in the Congo Basin, Amazonia, and Oceania. Indeed, of extant tribesmen, probably as many operate on this subsistence base as any other.

Widely distributed over the world, the practice of slash-and-burn agriculture is highly varied and in some locales marvelously intricate. Generally speaking, it is a seasonally regulated sequence of procedures designed to open up and bring under cultivation a patch of forest land. After one or two seasons of staple cropping the plot is neglected for years, usually with a view toward restoration of soil fertility through reversion to forest, following which the area may be cleared again for another cycle of cultivation and fallow. As a minimal definition, "slash-and-burn agriculture" applies where the customary interval of fallow exceeds the usual period of staple-crop cultivation.

Slash-and-burn cultivation goes under a variety of names: some local ones, such as *ladang* in Indonesia or *milpa* in Central America; some partially misleading ones, such as "shifting agriculture"; and some intellectually fashionable ones, such as "swidden cultivation," a North English term recently revived by anthropologists. "Shifting agriculture" is appropriate in reference to the short-term use of forest plots, but it should not be presumed that the land is inevitably exhausted in the process, and the people perennially forced to move on in quest of greener forests. Recent studies show that swiddening is not necessarily detrimental to soils or incompatible with stable village life—particularly in moister regions and in the absence of the population and political pressures normal to colonialism. Most "shifting agriculturalists" are able and content to reuse nearby plots of reverted, secondary forest (anyhow

---

[1] This procedure carries one special disadvantage. There is an inevitable temptation to deal only with those ecotypes involving a dominant, one-sided productive commitment, such as forest agriculture or pastoralism, though many tribes have mixed modes of livelihood. I do not want to obscure the range of variation, but I cannot adequately cope with it here. Let the student then beware of what follows and, one hopes, be stimulated to go beyond its simplicities.

[2] Cited in Harold C. Conklin, "The Study of Shifting Cultivation," *Current Anthropology*, II (1961), 27.

easier to clear than virgin forest) and thus remain sedentary for long periods. The "pioneering" of virgin land, entailing chronic relocation of settlements, is a minority practice among swidden cultivators.

Swidden agriculture is typically adjusted to a seasonal alternation of drier and wetter periods, with preparation of the field undertaken in a dry season and cultivation timed to catch the rains. The main tasks include selecting the site, cutting down forest growth, firing the accumulated debris, planting, weeding, and harvesting—perhaps also fencing and guarding against animal incursions. Local variations occur in all these practices. The extent to which the forest is cut away, for example, is more or less complete: undergrowth and thinner trees are generally taken down but larger trees are often left standing, though their branches may be pruned (pollarded), or the trees themselves killed by ringing the bark or firing the base. Fertilizers are not usually applied to a swidden field, except for the ashes of firing worked into the soil by rains. Deep tillage is likewise not characteristic of swidden farming. Seeds may be simply dropped in holes punched into the soil with a digging stick (e.g., rice planting in Southeast Asia); or they may be broadcast-sown over an area lightly turned by hoe (grain planting in Africa). Root crops are raised from cuttings, often in small mounds of heaped earth (e.g., yam planting in Oceania). The main staples of swidden agriculturalists include: manioc (originally in South American tropical forest; now widely distributed in the tropical world), maize (in the Americas; now also widely distributed), millet and sorghum (Africa), rice (Southeast Asia and Indonesia), sweet potato and yam (Oceania; now Africa and elsewhere), taro and banana (Oceania and Southeast Asia; now widespread).

A field may be principally devoted to one crop, such as rice or maize, but other plants are usually "intercropped" with the staple. Indeed, many different cultigens may be raised in the same plot: some staple and some secondary, some planted in the same season and some in successive seasons, so that the field yields regularly for over a year. Hanunóo swidden gardeners of the Philippines cultivate some 68 basic types of food plant (altogether about 280 specific subtypes), plus a number of useful non-food plants, and over 40 basic crop types have been observed growing at the same time in the same garden.[3]

Slash-and-burn is small-scale agriculture. The cleared plots are often an acre or less. In many regions one hectare (2.47 acres) under cultivation supplies a family of five to eight people for a year. Cultivation is "labor-intensive" —that is, heavily dependent on human effort, without benefit of plow or draft animals and involving only simple tools such as axes and machetes (nowadays) for clearing, hoe and digging stick for cultivating. An average adult might put in 500 to 1,000 or more man-hours/year in agricultural tasks. (This figure— though it excludes food preparation and other subsistence production—may constitute no particular advantage over the time spent by hunters and gatherers in food-getting.[4] Careful comparative study of swidden gardeners and hunters would probably bring into question the traditional view that the neolithic

[3] Harold C. Conklin, *Hanunóo Agriculture in the Philippines* (Rome: Food and Agriculture Organization of the United Nations, 1957), p. 147.

[4] Compare Frederick B. McCarthy and Margaret McArthur, "The Food Quest and the Time Factor in Aboriginal Economic Life," in C. P. Mountford, ed., *Records of the American-Australian Scientific Expedition to Arnhem Land: Anthropology and Nutrition*, Vol. 2 (Melbourne: Melbourne University Press, 1960), pp. 145–194.

"revolution" gave man relief from the food quest and "the leisure to build culture.") A large labor force, however, is not usually required for swidden farming: a single family will undertake many of the main operations on its own fields, perhaps with outside help for such tasks as clearing. And despite the primitive equipment, yields may be high in proportion to labor expended—higher than in certain systems of intensive cultivation.[5]

The principal disadvantage of swidden cultivation is the large amount of arable land required. With customary fallows of eight years, ten years, or longer, each community has to have much more land at its disposal than it has in cultivation at any given moment.[6] Gross population density is therefore often lower than that maintained by intensive plow or irrigation agriculture. The population density of forest cultivators is frequently less than 10 people/square mile. Settlement size is likewise restricted: villages larger on the average than 200–250 people are unusual in swidden areas.

Indeed local poplation growth may constitute a serious threat to swidden farming—a threat especially known to materialize in confined "native reserves," as in Africa. In the absence of free land for expansion, the increased need for food has to be met by shortening customary fallow periods, thus inhibiting full recuperation of plots. The equilibrium between man and nature is disturbed. Irreversible changes in soil and vegetation set in—the formation of hard soils deficient in organic compounds ("lateritization") and of tough grasses and sod—removing the land beyond local agricultural capabilities.

Slash-and-burn agriculture affords a richer material existence than mobile hunting-gathering, though perhaps not so much in consequence of a greater productivity of labor as of a greater stability of settlement. Wandering peoples must fix their living standards at what they can carry. A sedentary existence, however, allows accumulation of at least a modicum of domestic wherewithal: substantial housing, along with pottery, woven cloth, mats, and other neolithic knicknacks. Truly, a broad cultural advance on all fronts is sometimes fabricated from no more than slash-and-burn production—e.g., the lowland Maya, who thus display at a higher level a paradox analogous to the rich tribal cultures of Northwest Coast Indians established on a hunting-fishing-gathering base. But the main run of forest agriculturalists do not reach "high-culture" standards. They tend to be organized as simple segmentary tribes. For this mode of adaptation commonly maximizes local cleavages at the expense of regional organization. Capitalizing the tribal infrastructure, it lends itself to a decentralized system of autonomous communities rather than a pyramidal chiefdom.

Swidden agriculture has a centrifugal effect on the distribution of settlements, and a population dispersed through tropical forest is not well situated for political unification. Pioneering farmers may be able to gather in large settlements, but at the necessity of chronic outward movement toward virgin lands. Stable forest agriculture, on the other hand, requires ample reserve land and therefore a scattered deployment of people. Here the main alterna-

---

[5] Cf. D. E. Dumond, "Swidden Agriculture and the Rise of Maya Civilization," *Southwestern Journal of Anthropology*, XVII (1961), 301–316.

[6] This is the case if the community is to maintain continuous occupation. Obviously, if settlements and gardening sites are relocated after one or two agricultural cycles, the land requirements are likewise substantial.

tives are: (1) a pattern of small hamlets or homesteads diffused over the landscape, each surrounded by its subsistence lands; or (2) small villages of maybe 100–150 people separated from each other by wide cultivable areas.[7] Taken in conjunction with existing means of communication, this thin distribution of population is a political drawback. Except along navigable waterways, local groups may be condemned to forest isolation. The authority of any leader is then not readily extended beyond his own neighborhood, nor is it otherwise easy to coordinate the affairs of different villages or districts. Higher organization has to contend with an ecological blockade.

At the same time, and perhaps even more important, circumstances of production sharply set apart the village or neighborhood-community of forest agriculturalists. Regional specialization of production is usually limited, and each local group has the manpower and organization to tend to its own business. Land rights are correspondingly exclusive, set at the family, hamlet, lineage, or community level, or several of these simultaneously, but rarely at a higher level.

Add to this that continuous cultivation in secondary forest will not evoke any antithesis between sword and plowshare. On the contrary, cultivation may pass directly into intercommunity competition—over valuable land. The economic status-quo requires a balanced man-land ratio in each community, clearly a fragile equilibrium, easily upset by local variations in birth and death rates. Encroachment by larger groups on the garden-lands of smaller groups is not the only way to restore the balance, but it is at least a conceivable tactic, and the militant ethos of many forest tribes testifies some readiness to adopt it.[8] The effects on intercommunity relations are complicated, but on the whole this self-centered concern for *lebensraum* probably encourages local solidarity at the expense of tribalism. Friendly understandings with certain nearby communities could prove useful, both to curb competition and promote alliance against other groups. Even so, beyond this minimal sphere of peaceable relations, itself not entirely secure from dissension, the community is often set apart by its own interests from a hostile world, which very likely includes fellow-tribesmen.

Pastoral Nomadism

Pastoral nomadism is in fundamental ways the ecological converse of forest agriculture: an adaptation to open semi-arid grassland as opposed to tropical rain forest, a commitment to animal husbandry to the virtual exclusion of plant cultivation, and an economic basis rather of chiefdoms than of segmentary tribes. If the generalized mixed economy of early Near Eastern

---

[7] Somewhat larger villages might be maintained by a compromise involving seasonal occupation of hamlets near distant fields, with regroupment in the village after the harvest. But if a higher concentration of people is thus accommodated, the space between villages is probably also greater than usual.

[8] Cf. Andrew P. Vayda, "Expansion and Warfare among Swidden Agriculturalists," *American Anthropologist*, LIII (1961), 347–358. The wide distribution of corporate matrilineage organization among forest agriculturalists may be further connected to chronic competition. The women are a stable core of gardeners, perforce related to the land, as their mobile menfolk must be detached from it for their military adventures.

sites be taken as the neolithic prototype, pastoralism represents a specialized offshoot in the opposite direction from forest agriculture.

The classic locus of pastoral tribes is the transcontinental dry belt of Asia and Africa: Manchuria, Mongolia, Tibet, Turkestan, Iran, Arabia, the Sahara and its environs. Here live the most famous pastoralists, such as the Mongol and Turkic hordes of Inner Asia and the "Noble Bedouin" of Arabia. In attentuated form, pastoralism extends into the north Eurasian forest and tundra, a region dominated, from Lapland to Kamchatka, by reindeer herders. In Africa, pastoralists are distributed through the great arc of grassland north, east, and south of the forested Congo Basin: from peoples such as the Fulani of the West African savannah to the Turkana and Masai of East Africa, thence around to Southwestern Africa where the Hottentot, Herero and others practice a variant of East African husbandry.

This is, with forest agriculture, a major tribal ecotype. The herders of Inner Asia number in the millions. In Africa the area given to pastoralism is much greater than the total of cultivated land. At least one-tenth the people of the Southwest Asian mountains and plateaus are pastoral nomads, and one-fifth the population of Arabia. Pastoralism properly so-called, involving full commitment to herding to the neglect of agriculture, did not develop in pre-Columbian America, although in the post-contact era some people, such as the sheep-raising Navaho, did enter the pastoral fold.

Pastoralism is the negation of agriculture. But perhaps not in its origins, and often not in its existing forms, can pastoralism be understood apart from agrarian communities. Classic pastoralism, the highly mobile mounted nomadism of Inner Asia, appears to have developed around 1500–1000 B.C. as an offshoot of mixed farming.[9] The late date is intriguing. For thousands of years before, diversified neolithic economies had at many points approached the semi-arid Asian steppe, occupying transitional environments which favored emphasis on the animal side of the subsistence complex. Yet no extensive adaptation to the grassland seems to have been made, as if there were some impediment to a conclusive separation from the neolithic heartlands. Partly the reluctance may be attributable to the absence during all this time of suitable transport for humans, which large scale herding in the steppe requires: the horse was not ridden until late in the second millennium B.C., and the camel apparently not domesticated until then. But in another part, it may have been the absence of sufficient push from behind which, rendering continued occupation of the marginal economic zone unappealing, made even a semi-desert attractive. Contemplating the history of the ecologically-transitional border of China and interior Asia, Owen Lattimore was led to suggest that here the expansion of a dominant and exploitative Chinese civilization supplied the decisive force.[10] To take up mobile herding was for people of the border an act of resistance, even of freedom. "Where optimum conditions of

---

[9] I particularly refer here to extensive, mobile and mounted pastoralism. Smaller-scale and more sedentary herdsmen, without transport animals, may have appeared much earlier on the fringes of Southwest Asian neolithic developments.

[10] Owen Lattimore, *Inner Asian Frontiers of China* (New York: American Geographical Society, Research Series No. 21, 1951). See also, Lawrence Krader, "Culture and Environment in Interior Asia," in *Studies in Human Ecology* (Washington: Pan American Union, Social Science Monographs, III, 1957), 115–138.

pasturage adjoined minimum conditions of agriculture," Lattimore wrote, "the poor farmer could become a prosperous nomad by abandoning his under-privileged share of civilization and taking to the steppe." The general appli-cability of Lattimore's thesis is problematical. Pastoralism may have been invented more than once, but at least sometimes as a by-product of imperial civilization rather than a direct product of neolithic evolution.

So many peoples are loosely called "nomads" or "pastoralists" that it be-comes necessary to be specific about the practices denoted. Nomadic pastoral-ists are fully specialized herders, entirely devoted to the care of their numerous animals and the mobile life this entails. Their mobility and their specialized reliance on animals are mutually contingent: the herds must be moved from pasture to pasture, waterhole to waterhole, and the movement thus enjoined on people precludes attention to crops. Pastoralists engage in minimal amounts of agriculture, "true" pastoral nomads in none at all. In certain severe environ-ments and areas marginal to main centers of pastoralism, the people may depend heavily on a single animal species—the camel in northern Arabia, reindeer in Siberia, cattle in Southwestern Africa. The full pastoralism of Central Asia, however, encompasses a complex of animals—as of horses, cattle, camels, sheep, goats—with a herd balance nicely adjusted to local climatic and grazing conditions.

Everywhere, care of the herds demands frequent changes of camp and sometimes long marches. Some nomads range as many as 1,000 miles in an annual trek. As the old Chinese annal says, "their country is the back of a horse." But the migrations are not in fact aimless or boundless. Nomad tribes (or tribal subdivisions) do have countries: specific pastures and waterholes which come into season at various times and through which travel the people and their animals in a regular annual cycle.[11]

Nomadism is the most extensive of tribal economies. The human population is accordingly thinly distributed—although, given the degree of movement, communication and interaction among nomads may be disproportionately intense. For most of the year the people may travel in groups of 100–200, or fewer, and rarely, and then usually not for long, might they gather in larger numbers. Population densities range mainly between one and five people per square mile. In the rich steppe northwest of the Caspian Sea, the Kalmuk Mongols maintain an average density of about 18 per square mile; on the other hand, in parts of the Gobi Desert the nomadic density falls to 0.2 per square mile.[12]

People are not the only thing in short supply. Of the nomad it is truly said that his wealth is a burden. And it soon poses a contradiction to his mobility. An accumulation of worldly goods beyond a certain point restricts the pas-toralist's freedom of movement, thus reducing his ability to care for his stock and threatening his livelihood. Therefore, to take another line of Lattimore's,

---

[11] In certain sections of Southwest Asia, different nomad tribes, by arrangement, use the same pastures in succession; each has the right to certain pastures *at certain times.* See Fredrik Barth, "The Land Use Pattern of Migratory Tribes of South Persia," *Norsk Geo-grafisk Tidskrift,* XVII (1959–1960), 1–11.

[12] Some representative densities (persons per square mile) in Africa: Kenya Masai, 4.3; Tanganyika Masai, 2.0; Fulani, 2.4; Turkana, 3.3; Somali, 5.8; Mukogodo, 6.0; from Wil-liam Allan, *The African Husbandman* (Edinburgh: Oliver and Boyd, 1965), p. 309.

"the pure nomad is a poor nomad." Or if not exactly poor, he must go in for wealth that is portable and unbreakable. So if the pastoralist's conception of treasure is the shiny bangles that can be hung on a costume or inserted in his wife's coiffure, this is perfectly understandable.

Even as simple as their needs may be, pastoralists are characteristically unable to meet them directly from their own resources.[13] The livestock provide food (usually not so much in meat as milk or blood), dung for fuel, hides for leather utensils, wool or hides for clothing and perhaps housing. Livestock and livestock products are also marketable goods, and in this form may be just as critical to a pastoralist existence, inasmuch as the nomads must acquire by trade with agrarian communities the indispensable things they cannot themselves produce.

The pastoralist's relation to settled agriculturalists is like a happy marriage: the nomad can't stand the farmer, but can't live without him. The herdsman's famous contempt for the settled life in part reflects his own conflicts. As it were, he is thus reconciled to his poverty, and so preserves his freedom. Yet pastoral nomads are drawn to those they despise, as a matter of survival, and rarely exist apart from and without regular intercourse with settled communities. The pastoral and farming peoples of a given area comprise complementary economic sectors: the one exploiting local agricultural potentials, the other the husbandry possibilities of surrounding grasslands—and the two are then uneasily bound in relations of trade and tension.

Often the steppe does not afford a complete economy. It requires agricultural, craft, and industrial products. Without grains and other plant foods, the nomadic diet proves insufficient. Moreover, in poor grazing seasons (e.g., the height of summer in Arabia), the nomad may be unable to supply his livestock, and he is forced into town by their needs, and perhaps into some arrangements with local farmers for access to the stubble of harvested fields. Nor is the mobile nomadic life consistent with developed craft specialization. Pastoralists depend on towns for vital manufactures, ranging from metal utensils and weapons through clothing, footwear, and cloth for tents. The following observation, referring to Southwest Asia, indicates how deeply dependent on their agrarian neighbors pastoral nomads may be:

> Of the totality of objects contained in a nomad's home—be he a Kurd of
> West Iran or a Gujar in North Pakistan—only a small fraction have been
> produced by himself or a fellow nomad; and of the food such a family
> consumes in a year only a small fraction is pastoral products.[14]

---

[13] Students must be warned that controversy exists among our authorities concerning the ability of nomads to sustain themselves independently, apart from trade (or other economic relations) with agriculturalists. Without insisting this trade is a necessary or universal condition of pastoralism, I have come down here, perhaps too emphatically, on the "not self-sufficient" side. That is, I suppose the trade a normal condition.

[14] Fredrik Barth, "Nomadism in the Mountain and Plateau Areas of South West Asia," in *The Problems of the Arid Zone* (Paris: UNESCO, 1960), p. 345. Discussing Central Asia, Owen Lattimore observes that, "in spite of recurrent antipathy, there is a kind of symbiosis between every major group of pastoral nomads known in history and some settled society—perhaps more than one." (*Op. cit.*, pp. 333–334.) Apparent exceptions to the rule of symbiosis may be found in other areas; e.g., Siberian herders, or pastoralists of Southwest Africa such as the Herero.

Nomads exchange pastoral for town products, either with long-standing "trade friends" or in local markets. More sinister strategies are sometimes adopted: robbery, raid, exaction of tribute by force or—in the style of a protection racket—by threat of force. Still again, herders may have to deliver themselves into bondage to get what they need, hiring out as agricultural laborers or taking up tenant farming. Or the nomad may deal from economic strength: if he is rich he can buy town lands and collect rents in kind and coin.

Raid and trade are often alternative tactics of relationship between interdependent groups. The former may easily seem to the nomad the more feasible method of dealing with townsmen; so the town that one year welcomed a commercial exchange with men of the steppe discovers itself the next year prey to the same people—become now a pillaging horde, swooping down on the defenseless villagers like a wolf on the fold. The nomads' occasional desperation expresses another contradiction between wealth and mobility, here set on a higher, regional level. In exploiting townsmen by violence, nomads merely invert the ordinary relations. In peaceful trade, the pastoralist is at a disadvantage. He is the poorer. The exchange is more urgent to him than to the townsman. And he cannot hold out indefinitely for favorable terms for he must be off again, rather sooner than later, to the green pastures. On the other hand, though economically inferior to the settled people, the nomads are militarily superior. Born and bred to the saddle and to a career of raid and revenge, the pastoral nomad undertakes military training as a way of life. With practiced skill a nomad band can strike, steal, and disappear beyond hope of pursuit in the great waste, fading away without trace like a river running into desert sand. The townspeople often have nothing to match against these tactics, except it be a wall. Thus the economic relation between pastoralists and townsmen is inconsistent with the balance of force between them. Raid must often present itself to the nomads a better choice than trade, especially when they have suffered stock losses due to weather, sickness, or theft, and have little to exchange in any case.

Nomad tenancy and landlordism reflect other contradictions of the pastoral life, contradictions so deep as to detach men caught up in them from the steppe and force them to settle down. True, the poor nomad is the pure nomad, but if too poor he becomes a threat to his fellows' purity. If a family's livestock holdings fall below the minimum required for subsistence—a common happening given the uncertainties of husbandry and war—other families "chip in" to help only at some risk—that they might soon find themselves in the same straits. Nomads may have to be more selfish than agriculturalists. The social arrangements of pastoralists often inhibit responsibility for others' welfare, and poor families are thus driven by necessity into the town before they become a drag on the livestock-capital of everyone potentially concerned. In some areas, the flow of pastoralists into settled communities is augmented by the relatively high natural increase of nomad populations, whose dietary and sanitary practices are healthier than townspeople's. Meanwhile, rich pastoralists are having their own problems. Big herds are difficult to manage, and the owner, faced with the prospect of diminishing returns, may be inclined to invest his surplus in other kinds of property, such as town lands. The rich man then brings into play the contradiction between wealth and mobility. He too settles down: to oversee his holdings and enjoy the profits. This "sedentariza-tion" of the too-poor and the too-rich is a normal process in many areas, and is another facet of the interdependence of steppe and town.[15]

Thus, the pastoralist adaptation sets up complex relations with nature and with other societies. What are the effects on nomad social structure? Gen-erally: widespread cohesion, tribalism, and some centralization at higher levels. Pastoralists frequently develop chiefdoms.

The mode of production promotes relations between nomadic communities and their combination in greater "hordes"—given a sufficient animal and human density. Lawrence Krader's comparative study of Central Asian tribes indicates that degrees of political integration vary directly with population density, thus ultimately with the natural abundance of water and pasture. Peoples more favorably situated are able to build political structure through several levels of integration—along genealogical lines, in the manner of conical clans—and even to embark on grand imperial conquests and afford the priestly luxury of participation in great world religions. Poor nomads, however, are held to elementary political units, though their descent system may be the same in principle.[16]

Given the required density, a nomadic adaptation sets in motion certain forces of political cohesion. Communities enter into regional arrangements of internal peace, collective defense, and periodic redistribution of natural re-sources. They combine in regional or tribal confederations, and perhaps acknowledge a paramount chief. This despite the wandering hither and thither; in fact, partly because of it. Tribalism blunts the frequent collisions between neighboring camps and minimizes competition over pasture. Moreover, it bestows advantages in another sphere of pastoral conflict, the endemic cattle-raiding and counter-raiding of nomad life. We say "endemic" because livestock are vulnerable to disease and pastures to a capricious nature, but breeding herds back to full strength is a slow business, perhaps too slow to stave off bondage, sedentarization, or death. So instead, as the Bedouin put it, "raids are our agriculture." Cattle-raiding is of course divisive as well as self-perpetuating. But at the same time it encourages offensive and defensive alliances between communities, and allegiances to powerful men in a position to extend security and distribute booty. Finally—and this perhaps is the most important internal source of nomad cooperation—the annual cycles of neigh-boring groups have to be coordinated, lest they fail to distribute themselves in proper relation to pastoral resources. This often entails an annual allocation of pastures among neighboring communities, and perhaps also certain agree-ments with agrarian settlements or other nomad confederacies near the pro-jected pastoral routes. Clearly, decisions about migrations cannot be taken by a community in isolation. They have to be made in concert by leading men of neighboring camps, or else be made for and imposed upon the collection of communities by a paramount chief.

The adaptations of nomads to agrarian settlements have similar implica-

---

[15] Barth, *op. cit.*; and *Nomads of South Persia* (New York: Humanities Press, Oslo University Press, 1961).

[16] Lawrence Krader, "Ecology of Central Asian Pastoralism," *Southwestern Journal of Anthropology*, XII (1955), pp. 301–326; and "Principles and Structures in the Organiza-tion of the Asiatic Steppe Pastoralists," *op. cit.*, pp. 67–92.

tions: confederation and centralization of the herders. The town's wealth acts upon nomads as a magnet upon iron filings, not merely attracting them but bringing them together in the process. This cohesion is plainly functional where the pastoralists confront sedentary centers as military predators or political overlords. But even where they appear in town markets as peaceful traders, strong organization may have subtle advantages; e.g., as a covert threat favorably influencing rates of exchange on pastoral products. Besides, it is useful for the nomads to have a chiefly representative, perhaps permanently situated in the town, who will prosecute grievances that they in a necessarily brief stay cannot see through.

Meanwhile, the townsmen have a complementary need to treat with "persons of authority" among these wildmen. Like European *colons* in Africa or the Pacific, the first inclination of townspeople is to "find the chief"—a need so compelling that nomad chiefs may have to be invented if they do not already exist. A nomad polity is crystallized by outside pressure. As Fredrik Barth observes of Southwest Asian pastoralists:

> Where tribes had acephelous lineage organizations, as among some of the Pathan nomads, the authorities have not been able to deal through that organization, and have essentially created chiefs by insisting upon dealing with "persons of authority." Such persons could in the context of their own system be regarded as delegates speaking on behalf of lineage assemblies. But through the support they received from outside their position became more entrenched; and relations with sedentary centers have been a continual factor in changing tribal political organizations from the acephelous [i.e., segmentary] to the centralized type.[17]

The town's longing for a nomad chief is partly economic. The settled people too need someone through whom they can deal with the nomads in general and against whom they can lodge claims. (It is common in Southwest Asia to find nomad chiefs who are not nomadic by occupation but town-dwellers—and probably also graduates of Columbia University.) Moreover, influential chiefs can be used by townspeople to control the unruly men of the steppe. The town interferes in steppe politics, as China was wont to do on her northwest frontier, with a view toward neutralizing the border or creating a buffer of "friendly Indians." This may be dangerous. It involves subsidizing a certain degree of nomad organization and a certain measure of nomad leadership—yet not too much of either, lest it bring a dragon to the city gates.

The tendency of pastoralists to form chiefdoms is in any case often not as complete as it might be. Ethnographers speak of a certain instability in nomadic polities, which they formulate in various ways: as a conflict between kinship and contract, between descent and "individualism," or (in reference to the highest offices) between hereditary succession and "usurpation." One source of weakness in the community infrastructure we have already detected: the necessity to limit social solidarity and thereby extensive economic responsibilities, so that impoverished families are sloughed off before they become a drain on the community's livestock. Individual dealing in town markets, which demands personal accumulation of the wherewithal of trade at

---

[17] Barth, "Nomadism in the Mountain and Plateau Areas of South West Asia," p. 349.

the expense of local charity, would tend to have a similar fracturing effect.

Again, the nomads' militarism can compromise social principles by expediency, at any and all levels of organization. Families, camps, or entire tribal sections have to seek refuge where they can find it. Although common descent may be conceived the proper basis of collaboration, exigency may decree otherwise. An *ad hoc* combination of forces that provides security is preferable to a genealogical alliance that is only morally correct. Militarism also gives scope to the personal achievement of power, rewarding with followers those who can reward followers. But such men are not necessarily chiefs by birthright. On one hand, this means that charismatic leaders usurp or create official status rather than inherit it; on the other, that their henchmen and subordinate groups may be attached by personal allegiance rather than kinship rule, recruited to the lord's service by the promise of glory and booty, or the fear of losing such as they have.

The "disorderliness" of the nomad chiefdom appears then in two dimensions. First, the chiefdom is only insubstantially based on a corporate descent system, such as a conical clan. Lineage affiliation makes concessions to contractual relations: bondage, clientage, vassalage, and blood brotherhood. Second, a symmetrical political pyramid, with major and minor chiefs heading up greater and lesser subdivisions, is frequently not achieved. Power tends to be concentrated at the top, with subordinate groups standing rather equally and severally under the paramount.

Hunting, Fishing, and Gathering Tribes

The western fringe of North America from California to southern Alaska was occupied in aboriginal times by tribes without agriculture or husbandry. Similarly, certain southwestern New Guinea tribes have relied on food collection rather than food production. The combination of tribal structure and hunting-fishing-gathering production is, however, exceptional. It usually depends on the existence of one or two surpassingly abundant wild foods —e.g., fish (especially salmon) in the American Northwest, acorns in California, sago in New Guinea—which when taken in their season afford something like an agricultural harvest. It might be said of these people that they practice a "natural agriculture."

Still, in praising nature's bounty we should not slight the people's competance. By unusually fine techniques they capitalize on their unusual opportunities. No mean skill or knowledge is incorporated in the procedures by which California tribes rendered edible the naturally poisonous acorn, or in the numerous methods of taking and storing salmon, sea mammals, and other foods practiced by Northwest Coast Indians. The productivity of the latter tribes, especially, would occasion no embarrassment in comparison with agricultural peoples of native North America.

Hunting-gathering tribes may also enjoy as much material comfort as the run of "neolithic" tribesmen. Many of the best wood-carvers of the primitive world are tribal hunters and gatherers, such as the Asmat of New Guinea and the Northwest Coast Indians. The California Indians are generally awarded the accolade for basketry among primitive (or for that matter, any) peoples. Associated with these achievements is a semi-sedentary existence—in "seasonal villages" at least—and, sometimes, year-round village life.

Population densities of tribal hunter-gatherers likewise measure up to neolithic standards. The aboriginal population density of California was about as high as any region north of Mexico, including agricultural regions.[18] Northwest Coast Indians were not far behind. Villages of the Asmat (New Guinea) range up to 2,000 people. This, however, may be ten to twenty times the average for hunting-gathering tribes, whose settlements generally are comparable to those of forest agriculturalists'.

Also like forest agriculturalists, the small hunting-gathering community is inclined to be independent. Not that it is socially isolated. The village is linked by kinship and other relations to other villages of the tribe, and uncertainties of food-collecting turn these connections into providential causeways of material aid. But the same uncertainties hamper the political unification of such communities, and for that matter the internal integration of each community.

The natural food supplies available to local groups of hunting-gathering tribes are subject to much seasonal and annual variation. The community at one time well off may find itself at another beset with serious shortages. Affording no secure fund of power by disposition of which a "core area" might dominate surrounding settlements, these uncontrollable variations afford no effective basis for centralized regional polities. Along the Northwest Coast, chieftains of "noble" birth were influential in the several lineages ("houses") and villages. But none could continuously maintain supremacy over a tribal region, any more than the salmon would run in abundance year in and year out in the streams claimed by any one chief.[19] Moreover, the mobility of the hunter, here more restricted than usual but nevertheless periodically evident, infects an otherwise stable order with an underlying turbulence. Families disperse to favored food-getting haunts in certain seasons, putting themselves out of touch and beyond central control. A long-term decline in local food resources induces permanent emigration, undermining the support of would-be chiefs and changing radically the local and regional correlation of forces.

Thus, despite the dense population it may support, food-collecting by its inherent insecurities unhinges a tribal structure. It continuously disturbs political codification both of the local community and the regional congeries of communities. Local groups tend to be less coherent and less solidary than in agricultural settings, where specific resources exploited over long periods give anchorage to strong corporate formations. At the same time, regional polities (as opposed to regional sociabilities) are not easily developed, and if developed remain comparatively unstructured. In general, if not invariably, the tribes of food collectors are amorphous segmentary systems.

---

[18] A. L. Kroeber, *Cultural and Natural Areas of Native North America* (Berkeley and Los Angeles: University of California Press, 1947). Kroeber's figures for California were underestimates. According to Baumhoff, densities of California tribes ranged up to 11.12 per square mile; Martin A. Baumhoff, *Ecological Determinants of Aboriginal California Populations* (Berkeley and Los Angeles: University of California Press, 1963).

[19] Wayne Suttles, "Affinal Ties, Subsistence, and Prestige among the Coast Salish," *American Anthropologist*, LXII (1960), 296–305; Andrew P. Vayda, "A Re-examination of Northwest Coast Economic Systems," *Transactions of the New York Academy of Sciences*, Series II, Vol. XXIII (1961), 618–624.

Equestrian Hunters

The Sioux, Cheyenne, Comanche, and other tribes of the Great Plains almost exhaust popular conceptions of the American Indian. Today's stereotype of "an Indian," that intrepid mounted warrior of painted mien and feathered bonnet, was characteristic of the Plains and of no other area of America. Before the coming of the white man, this kind of Indian did not exist anywhere. The florescence of Plains culture was a fugitive episode, lasting only from the introduction of the horse to the extinction of the buffalo, altogether less than 300 years; and these decisive opening and closing events, as well as the trade that subsidized tribal history in all the time between, were "benefits" of European civilization. Nor are there many ecological parallels elsewhere: an analogous post-Columbian development in Patagonia, of which less is known, and a somewhat similar pattern of hunting from reindeer-back in Siberia (the Northern Tungus). But perhaps the best analogies come from pastoral tribes on one side, and pure hunting tribes on the other. For the Plains adaptation, combining horse-herding, buffalo-hunting, raid and trade in an interdependent complex, combines essential features of these adaptations.

Like nomadism, Plains life was peripatetic. But the mobility was dictated more by hunting free herds of bison than pasturing domesticated herds of horses. The buffalo followed a natural cycle of concentration and dispersal, "blackening the Plains" in huge masses during their late summer rutting season, then scattering in smaller herds in winter and spring. The Indians responded with a parallel social cycle, coming together for tribal ceremonies and communal hunts in late summer, then breaking up in smaller bands (or still smaller kindred groups) for ordinary hunting. At the peak of concentration the entire tribe (or a major tribal section) assembled—perhaps a few thousand people—but the bands and kindreds that otherwise went their separate ways comprised only small fractions of the tribal whole.

The economy was land-extensive, and the population density accordingly low, substantially below one person per square mile in the southern Plains.[20] As is the lot of pastoral nomads, constant movement also restricted the quantity and character of Plains Indians' wealth. They made no pottery, cloth, or basketry, and developed only weakly manufactures in wood, stone, and bone; but relied instead on leather products and metal trade goods, and lavished most attention on their beaded, bangled, and befeathered costumes.

Reminiscent of nomadism was the continuous posture of belligerence toward traditional enemies, and the horse-thievery of everyday life. Conflict among the Indians was constantly stimulated by differential access to European goods, and periodically exacerbated by radical relocations of European trade posts and changes in their demands for Indian goods. From an early period, the several tribes had unequal opportunities to acquire horses and guns—horses came into the Plains mainly from Spanish settlements in the south, and guns from French and English traders in the northeast. Certain

---

[20] Jerrold E. Levy, "Ecology of the South Plains," in Viola E. Garfield, ed., *Symposium: Patterns of Land Utilization and Other Papers* (Seattle: American Ethnological Society, 1961), pp. 18-25.

tribes were thus empowered to expand at the expense of their poorer neighbors, while those beleaguered were forced to adopt all available means of preservation, from chicanery to alliance against the strong. But suddenly the strategic calculus would change, as when the opening of the Missouri to steamboats also opened a massive trade in buffalo hides. Tribes that had risen to ascendancy on a wave of superior armaments were now forced to retreat before people they had previously driven before them. Any military equilibrium was likely to be thus upset as soon as it was established, and a wrath nurtured by decades of defeat made victims of onetime victors.[21]

The selective pressures favored tribal cohesion, as among pastoral nomads. But also analogous to the nomad condition, and even more similar to the situation of hunters, formal organization of this cohesion was hampered by continuous economic instability. Their movements and meetings within the same territory enjoined tribal solidarity on Plains bands; and warfare too put a premium on intratribal coherence, even intertribal alliance. Yet tribes that had had lineages and clans before their entrance on the Plains now found these undermined. Nor did any develop a true, centralized system of chieftainship.

Plains bands were loose congeries of kinsmen, easily joined and easily left, as fluctuations in horse-holdings or hunting chances might dictate. The same capriciousness haunted pivotal big-men,[22] whose influence was contingent on the impermanent successes of warfare and horse-raising. Thus tribal unity was not effected by a segmentary set of lineages and lineage chiefs: it was fostered by cross-cutting associations, such as military societies and age-grades, and worked out in councils of leading men. Plains tribes did organize at higher levels, but with minimum formality. They produced the outlines of chiefdoms, but not the inner structure.

Intensive Agriculture

Oasis irrigation was probably one of the earliest forms of agriculture in the Near East, and several varieties of irrigation were known to peoples of the Mesoamerican neolithic. Adapted to the great river systems of Egypt, Mesopotamia, and other strategic centers, irrigation became eventually the technical basis of many archaic civilizations. Simpler types of hydraulic agriculture persisted, however, in the primitive world: in arid regions, or even tropical climes where the crops raised (e.g., rice or taro) would benefit from heavy applications of water. In the American Southwest, small-scale irrigation or flood-water farming (using controlled spring or stream run-offs) provided the mainstay of the Pueblo Indians. The complex adaptations of Polynesians, which included fishing, tree-culture, and forest agriculture, often emphasized stream irrigation of taro, notably in Hawaii, where creative techniques of ditching, damming and terracing were responsible for a substantial proportion of native subsistence.

---

[21] Frank Raymond Secoy, *Changing Military Patterns on the Great Plains*, American Ethnological Society Monographs, No. XXI (1953).

[22] In the ethnographic literature, Plains' leaders are styled "chiefs"; in sociological type they are big-men of the sort described in Chapter 2.

These are intensive methods of food production. The irrigation waters replenish fertility, allowing continuous or nearly continuous cropping. The return to labor expended is not necessarily higher than in slash-and-burn, but yields relative to arable land are much greater. Not obliged to keep the greater portion of their land uncultivated and in reserve, irrigation agriculturalists can maintain relatively dense populations and relatively large settlements. Single pueblos might exceed 1,500 people in the Southwest U.S.,[23] and the population density of the Pueblo area was the highest in aboriginal America north of Mexico. Hawaiians, on the other hand, did not live in villages proper, but their homesteads were often concentrated in the lower valleys and overall density was high—e.g., about 25/square mile in the "Big Island" (Hawaii), despite its great stretches of non-arable land.

The carefully constructed relation to nature involved in hydraulic agriculture suggests also certain social constructions. For instance, a stable substratum of local groups, firmly attached to the land and perhaps formally constituted as proprietary lineages. A large measure of cooperation is required here— within and between these groups—in connection with the upkeep of the irrigation system and the distribution of water to individual fields. Some coherence at secondary and higher levels of organization also seems called for, if only by the dense association of many people.

The well-known "hydraulic thesis" elaborated by K. A. Wittfogel[24] is relevant at this juncture. Wittfogel argues that an extensive and centralized political system is a functional specification of irrigation on the grand scale. Mass labor must be mobilized for the construction, maintenance, and flood-protection of great waterworks. A certain organization of people is therefore implied: a society divided into a powerful bureaucratic sector and a subject peasantry, the whole dominated by an exalted ruler of unlimited authority. The complete political expression of large-scale irrigation is a despotic "Oriental Society," such as pharaonic Egypt, ancient Peru, or historic China. By "backward" extrapolation, the incomplete or primitive analogue would be a centralized chiefdom, such as the Hawaiian. The reliance upon irrigation in some Polynesian chiefdoms does give modest support to these contentions— but even the Hawaiians drew on a diversified technology, and the Polynesian polity cannot be understood as a simple consequence of irrigation.

Involving limited construction and small opportunity for water control, flood-water farming and the other simple hydraulic schemes of the American Southwest make fewer organizational demands than large-scale irrigation. A strong central authority is not technically required and, indeed, given the level of production in the Pueblo area would be difficult to support. But this political simplicity is no special blessing; it is a special problem. Many people are perforce concentrated in the areas open to cultivation. Here is a dense *ecological* association—in the Hopi pueblos, people living on top of one another—but no centralized *political* association: a society operating at tight quarters yet capable of only moderate formations of leadership and polity. In

---

[23] Zuni pueblo was 1,700 in 1915–1916, 2,252 in 1951. Hopi villages now average about 300 people, but some pueblos are nearly juxtaposed and estimates for the seventeenth and eighteenth centuries indicate a greater population. See Fred Eggan, *Social Organization of the Western Pueblos* (Chicago: University of Chicago Press, 1950).

[24] Karl A. Wittfogel, *Oriental Despotism* (New Haven: Yale University Press, 1957).

the Pueblo villages, discrete clan sections hold independent shares of the irrigable land; and there is no organization more inclusive than the village, though the next town may be just down the mesa. Anthropologists testify to a continuous undertone of bickering in the pueblos, which in a crisis may surface as bitter factionalism. The community breaks apart: the people who "don't like it here" go somewhere else.

To those whose education has included Ruth Benedict's *Patterns of Culture*,[25] the deeper turbulence of Pueblo life will come as a surprise. The Pueblos' reputation for peacefulness—their "Apollonian" noncompetitiveness —is well documented. But this ideological insistence on harmony, this trained repression of conflict, has to be understood dialectically. It compensates for a lack of direct political means; it is one way they overcome the underlying social cleavages. Another of the Pueblos' moral equivalents of politics, perhaps the most important, is their intense ceremonialism. The well-being of the people and crops is conceived dependent on an annual cycle of rituals, one following hard upon the last, and no ritual invocation of the gods can succeed without peace on the mesa and good will toward men. Each clan section, furthermore, controls the paraphernalia of one or more of the ceremonies. Each is therefore dependent for its existence on the other clans. The coherence that is constrained by ecology, yet not achieved in economy or polity, is asserted on the religious level as a ceremonial division of labor.

This adaptation of the cultural system, the summoning up of ideological reserves when first-line institutions of defense prove insufficient, is not unique, though it is expressed differently in other contexts. Often enough in the course of colonial subjugation, colonized peoples resort to a religious cult in their struggle against foreign devils. Cultures, like soldiers, find gods in foxholes.

Intercultural Adaptation

Our discussion of tribal ecotypes has been uneven in important respects. Note that the sections on pastoral nomads and equestrian hunters paid considerable attention to relationships between the tribes and neighboring peoples. Adaptation to a certain cultural environment was perceived as consequential to pastoral nomads as their adaptation to a grassland. But though the nomads were thus seen under *cultural* as well as *natural selection* most of the other tribal types were treated in isolation, apart from any cultural context, as if the adaptation to nature was alone significant. Clearly this procedure is historically deficient. With few exceptions, tribesmen everywhere are in contact with outsiders, sometimes quite different from themselves, and this engagement in an intercultural field influences local tribal organizations. Involved in a regional division of labor, pastoral nomads' interaction with other peoples may be in some sense more necessary than usual, but it is not necessarily more compelling in its effects.

So to the previous discussion of tribal adaptations to nature I should append here another, at least of equal length, on the relations of tribes to coexisting societies and the modifications in organization thus occasioned. Unfortunately,

[25] Ruth Benedict, *Patterns of Culture* (Boston: Houghton Mifflin, 1934).

this has been a neglected branch of ecological research, and little more can be presented to the student now than what to expect from it.

One *need* not expect that tribesmen become like their neighbors as a result of prolonged contact. Too much should not be made of the "acculturation" studies once in vogue, which emphasized the intense cultural diffusion accompanying colonialism and the inevitable Westernization of captive primitive societies. The interaction of tribal peoples may produce more *complementarity* than similarity in cultural configuration, particularly when staged against a backdrop of natural contrasts. The tribes differentiate by adaptation to nature and to each other, simultaneously and to their mutual advantage.

Melanesia affords classic examples, especially around the peripherae of the larger islands such as New Guinea, where successive differences in environment marching inland from shore to mountain are seized upon and capitalized in the lifeways of adjacent tribes. Coastal fishing peoples and "bush" taro gardeners—perhaps also riverine or swampland sago gatherers, upland sweet-potato cultivators and plains yam-growers—exist side by side and in economic symbiosis. Or, several island communities, each naturally endowed to produce certain crops or crafts, are linked together in a critical overseas trade network. The latter diversity may engender still more diversity. The local division of labor opens a niche for sailing-trading peoples, such as the Manus of the Admiralty Islands, who thereupon play the Phoenecian middlemen to a primitive *mare nostrum*. Clearly the success of all the tribes in such a regional *ecosystem* depends on preserving, or even magnifying, the differences between them—on emphasizing the diversity of their adaptations.

Conflict as well as cooperation (and the two need not be mutually exclusive) leaves its impress on tribal organization. The effects of external hostilities on internal structures depend upon many circumstances: the mode of competition, the cultural character of the antagonists, their respective levels of development—just to cite more obvious elements of the competitive calculus. A warfare of equals, tribe against tribe, tends to consolidate each at some high level, as in the instance of Plains Indians. But given a fundamentally segmentary organization, the movement toward confederation is often incomplete and sometimes more apparent among successful predators than among their prey.[26] Divisions within the enemy's camp help perpetuate one's own weaknesses. The tribe overcomes its local cleavages only so much as it must to prevail militarily, and in the absence of sustained opposition the normal separatist tendencies are periodically free to reassert themselves.

The case is different when a tribe is up against a superior organization, say a powerful chiefdom or a kingdom. Here the opposition is more extensive, dangerous, and continuous, and a like countervailing organization of the tribe becomes a minimal demand of existence. The chiefdoms formed by pastoral nomads in contention with agrarian centers in Southwest Asia or along the Chinese border are examples in point. As we have noted, it bears upon the organization of such chiefdoms that they are not entirely *sui generis* but crystallized by external pressure. The body politic may then retain features of a primitive organism, covered by a protective exoskeleton of chiefly authority

[26] Cf. Marshall D. Sahlins, "The Segmentary Lineage: An Organization of Predatory Expansion," *American Anthropologist*, LXIII (1961), 322–345.

but fundamentally uncomplicated and segmental underneath. That is to say, a structural gap appears between the central chieftainship and underlying local groups. The latter are not compounded in pyramidal fashion as major and minor subdivisions under representative chiefs of different rank. They comprise instead an undifferentiated stratum, each group separately deferring to the chieftainship, which is itself established as much in relation to an outside power as to the tribal substructure. Practically untouched by principles of rank and chiefly authority, local groups persist then as simple neolithic formations, almost as a different historic epoch, while the chiefly stratum, differentiated in style and values by its connections with a more sophisticated tradition, seems almost an intrusive element in the tribal body. Indeed, in a number of African tribes juxtaposed to greater kingdoms, the local authorities (such as they are) are foreign, or at least validate their superiority by a tradition of descent from neighboring royalty.

Tribes do not always respond to powerful neighbors by thrusting forward a chief and unifying behind him. It may prove the better part of valor to become invisible: to fragment into small, unobtrusive groups in such scattered disarray as to hardly constitute a threat to anyone, certainly not worth bothering with, if not altogether lost to sight. Some Middle Eastern tribes appear to hide out this way in a sea of more advanced peoples, interspersed among the latter as tiny islets of distinctive background and custom. Rarely do they settle or gather in provocative numbers, though the people in all may run into the thousands. Then again, a tribe may take shelter from superior cultural forces by running off into the forest in small and mobile communities. The Amahuaca, swidden cultivators of eastern Peru, appear to have adopted this strategy:

> The known history of the Amahuaca, imperfect though it is, has been one of external attack by other more powerful Indian tribes and by rubber gatherers, and internal feuding on a considerable scale. Small community size and frequent movement of settlements would have the effect of making communities more difficult to locate. They would afford some measure of protection and provide the best chance for survival. Thus, while there is no conclusive evidence for it, the recurrent moving of the Amahuaca may be interpreted as an ecological adaptation to conditions of great insecurity.[27]

Social fragmentation of another kind—in some ways deeper, though hardly manifest in the compact appearance of the tribal commune—has been known to accompany a people's adaptation to a commercial world. In the hinterlands of Southeast Asia—the outer islands of Indonesia and mountain regions of the mainland—live tribal groups, seemingly ordinary forest agriculturalists, but in fact unusual in that lower as well as higher levels of organization are relatively unintegrated. The local community is not only set apart from others, it is itself divided at the household level. Families tend to go their own way, quite solidary in themselves, but often not recognizing common lineage ties

---

[27] Robert Carneiro, "Shifting Cultivation among the Amahuaca of Eastern Peru," *Völkerkundliche Abhandlungen*, Vol. 1, Niedersachsisches Landmuseum Hannover (1964), 16.

with, or serious economic responsibilities for, co-villagers. True, each family is bound to others by consanguineal or affinal relationships, but the community is more an aggregate than a corporation, limited in collective functions, amorphous in composition and subject to frequent changes in membership. This decentralized or "atomized" condition is not historically confined to Southeast Asia: it appears in North America after European contact—e.g., among Northeast Woodland tribes such as the Ojibway.

The atomizing forces are external to the tribe. They penetrate the tribal hinterland from main centers of political development and trade, smashing the internal bonds of the primitive molecule and orienting the elementary household units outward, principally by the force of economic attraction. Internal relations are especially weakened where people market surpluses of their staple food—as the Lamet of Laos or the Iban of Borneo, who export hill rice for metal tools and other necessities, and for silk clothing, brass gongs, and other luxuries. To engage in this trade a family must painfully accumulate a food surplus, and to do so entails also a minimum of gratuitous generosity toward co-villagers, however straightened their circumstances. Discounting internal sociabilities is a functional demand of external trade. Otherwise, given that some families are sometimes short of rice, those who could afford it might be inclined to share with those in need, reducing everyone to the same level of discomfort and preventing anyone from getting brass gongs.

Not only is lineage and community organization thus debilitated, but also leadership, which remains undernourished and unable to provide a counter-force to the centrifugal effects of trade. From a comparative perspective what is lacking is that no one is able or willing to dispense aid and generate loyalties locally, nor could anyone command the resources of other households for such a purpose. Therefore, people are ratable only by their conspicuous consumption of trade goods, a display of prestige items which has as its necessary ante-cedent a concealment (or at least a reservation) of subsistence items. Yet invidious consumption by itself lacks the political effect of distributing comfort to those in need. Prestige goods may awe people but do not obligate them, and no prestigious rich man can overcome the commercial spoliation of community relations.

Four Social Structures

The last chapter, considering various types of adaptation, pondered also some general relationships between ecology and the tribal structure. Here, in discussing details of the latter, varieties of kinship and descent, we enter into the deeper mysteries of cultural anthropology.

It is customary to begin at the lowest levels, with interpersonal and familial relations, and then move upward to the major kinship and descent groups. I prefer to reverse the procedure: to avoid certain presumptions in it that are quite natural but perhaps equally misleading. Beginning at the infrastructure makes the larger kinship system seem a derivation of the smaller, a working out of fundamental principles established first on the interpersonal plane. Now as the natives see it, that does happen to be the way the world is constructed, but only, I think, because the world *is* better constructed—that is, society functions more smoothly—if they see it that way. As outsiders we are given the privilege of making sense of the tribal inner life from the larger configuration in which it is embedded. Then one perceives what no one within the system is allowed to suspect, that the superstructure imposes itself, sometimes quite arbitrarily, on the character of the family and the "primary" relationships.

Major Descent Groups

The tribe is a constellation of communities and relations between communities. The main elements of this structure are in substance major groupings of kinsmen. Descent groups in particular often comprise the nucleii of tribal sections; certain types of descent group can provide a framework for the entire tribal organization.

Major descent groups are organized on various principles. Descent may be matrilineal, patrilineal, or cognatic (nonunilineal); a single tribe can even combine functionally distinct matrilineal and patrilineal groups in a "system of double descent." Again, descent groups may be dispersed or localized, ranked or egalitarian, exogamous, endogamous, or agamous. Rather than consider these design features in isolation, I prefer to take up some of the common empirical combinations, and the tribal configurations of descent groups thus established.

Conical Clan

The conical clan, we already know, is a main strategy of chiefdom organization (see pp. 24–25 and Fig. 2.2).

The conical clan is a ranked and segmented common descent group. Genealogical seniority is the first rule of rank, and it holds throughout the clan: individuals of the same lineage are graded by their respective distance from the lineage founder; equivalent lineage branches are likewise ranked according to the position of their respective founders in the clan genealogy. Priority goes to the first-born son of first-born sons, and a different rank is ascribable to every member of the clan, precisely in proportion to his genealogical distance from the senior line.

In Polynesia, Inner Asia, and most places where it exists, the conical clan is in principle patrilineal. The affiliation of persons and lineage segments within the clan is expressed in the idiom of common descent in the paternal line, especially in contexts of opposition to like groups, and by way of distinction from like groups. But if you looked closely, you would probably discover that some men boast of rank derived from a maternal ancestor; and some claim membership in a clan by virtue of descent from a female member of it. The conical clan is often *in fact* cognatic, if *in ideology* agnatic (patrilineal). Any clan is likely to include "accessory branches" derived from women born of the clan.

Conical clans are typically neither exogamous nor endogamous. Chiefs are wont to marry close relatives, perhaps within the clan, an arrangement that satisfies their ideas of their own nobility and maintains the structure of elitism.

People of the same clan may be scattered in different parts of the tribal territory. But where extensive chiefdoms are constructed on conical clan lines, each clan usually has a regional appanage, a district in which it is supreme and over which the clan chief presides. Subdivisions of the district are similarly associated with branches of this clan and are headed-up by lineage chieftains. So empowered in the district, which is its main focus, the conical clan presents itself simultaneously as a descent group and a unit of political order. The tribe is made up of one or several such clans, arranged in one or (usually) several independent chiefdoms.

Segmentary Lineage Systems

These duplicate many features of conical clan organization. But in comparison with the latter, segmentary lineage systems are politically under-developed and are found rather in segmentary tribes than in chiefdoms.[1] The Nuer of the Eastern Sudan and the Tiv of Nigeria are the classic segmentary lineage systems. The following observations on Tiv lineage organization suggest the points of resemblance to conical clans:

> The lineage whose apical ancestor is some three to six generations removed from living elders and who are associated with the smallest discrete territory (*tar*) I call the minimal segment . . . it can vary in population from 200 people to well over a thousand. . . . The territory of a minimal segment adjoins the territory of its sibling minimal segment. Thus, the lineage comprising two minimal segments also has a discrete territory, and is in turn a segment of a more inclusive lineage, and of its more inclusive territory. In [Fig. 4.1], the whole system can be seen: the father or founder of segment *a* was a brother of the founder of segment *b*. Each is a minimal segment today, and each has its own territory. The two segments taken together are all descended from *1*, and are known by his name—the children of *1*. In the same way, the territory of lineage *1*, made up as it is of the combined minimal territories *a* and *b*, combines with the territory of lineage *2*, made up of the combined minimal territories of *c* and *d*, to form territory A, occupied by lineage segment A, all descended from a single ancestor "A." This process is extended indefinitely right up to the apex of the genealogy, back in time to the founder who begot the entire people, and outwards in space to the edges of Tivland. The entire 800,000 Tiv form a single "lineage" (*nongo*) and a single land called *Tar Tiv*. The geographical position of territories follows the genealogical division into lineages.[2]

Decentralized and egalitarian, a segmentary lineage system is like a conical clan only in outline; in substance and function it is quite different.

The lineage segments are not ranked. Indeed, no standing organization or leadership exists above the level of the autonomous minimal segment (*Lineages a, b, c,* etc., in Fig. 4.1). The great superstructure of lineage relations above the minimal segment is only an alliance network, brought into play during conflicts between the functioning minimal groups. This superstructure is a politics of "complementary opposition": in any serious dispute between

---

[1] I use "segmentary lineage system" in narrow reference to configurations of autonomous lineage-communities between which, however, higher-order lineage relations prevail and are enlisted (through "complementary opposition") for temporary alliances. There is no popular inclination among anthropologists to so restrict the use of the term. (See Sahlins, "The Segmentary Lineage: An Organization of Predatory Expansion.")

[2] Paul Bohannan, "The Migration and Expansion of the Tiv," *Africa,* II (1954), 3.

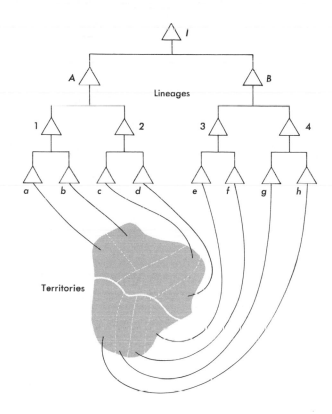

Figure 4.1. Segmentary lineage system (after Paul Bohannan, "The Migration and Expansion of the Tiv," Africa, II (1954), 3.

members of different minimal lineages, all outside groups more closely related to one contestant than the other take the side of their nearer kinsmen, and the issue is then joined between the highest order lineages thus involved. For example, an argument between Lineages *a* and *b* (Fig. 4.1) would remain just that, an argument between "brother" segments; but a dispute between Lineages *a* and *c* is transposed to a dispute between *1* and *2*, as minimal Lineage *b* joins *a* against *c* and minimal Lineage *d* joins *c* against *a*. In the same way, conflict between minimal Lineages *a* and *e* is translated into conflict between the higher-order Lineages A and B. But, and this is important, such higher-order lineages as A or B do not stand alone and as such. They do not have internal functions. They are organized solely in opposition to equivalent segments, and when the opposition that brought them into existence is put in abeyance, so are they: the higher lineage dissolves and the minimal segments carry on without reference to each other. Any pivotal leader fortunate enough to emerge during the period of intergroup dispute likewise now sinks back into local importance, if not into complete oblivion, without authority over brother lineages.

Here we have neither chieftainship nor regional polities, but only the capacity to fashion temporary versions of these in a time of stress. The segmentary lineage is a functional analogue of the conical clan within the limits prescribed by underdeveloped conditions. It is, as it were, a substitute for the continuous integration at higher levels that segmentary tribes are unable to maintain. By one theory, the segmentary lineage system is an adaptive response to opportunities of expansion provided by the existence of weak tribes in nearby desirable territories.[3] It is an organization of predation, facilitating intrusion against neighboring garden-variety tribesmen whose own fragmented condition proves in the showdown a fatal weakness. There is a built-in dynamism to segmentary lineage systems, and in a world of tribes a definite tactical advantage. Complementary opposition encourages the displacement of competition outward, away from "brother" lineages toward the most distant available enemy, against whom maximum force will be massed, as brother lineages join then in the good fight. By this logic, foreigners are clearly the best enemies to have. As Paul Bohannan reports of the Tiv, every lineage segment that does not actually adjoin foreigners knows "just which lineages they 'follow' (*chir*), and—though they are likely to push or shove (*kpolom*)— they will assist those in front to take over from foreigners." [4] In the confrontation with other tribes, it becomes "all of us" against "them," where "all of us" is a maximal lineage (or all Tiv thereabouts) while "them" is only a few of them.

Territorial Clans

The territorial clan may also have been conceived in violence. In the densely-populated New Guinea Highlands, the main ethnographic locus of this organization, the clans are frequently joined in struggles for land—although here it is principally internecine strife between blocs of the same "people," and principally a warfare of position rather than of massive invasion.

The New Guinea Highlands clan is a patrilineal, exogamous, descent group. The clan claims and defends a definite territory, within which most adult men of the group reside and make up the core of an autonomous community. Ethnic boundaries are usually vague, but it is clear enough that the people are divided into independent local groups, each a few square miles in extent and a few hundred or so in population. Certain clans of a region, however, may also consider themselves remotely related, with a common ancestor "from way back." They comprise a brotherhood of clans, a *phratry*. While clans of the same phratry should not war on each other but rather make a common cause if one is attacked, the automatic principle of complementary opposition is not in operation here.

New Guinea territorial clans raise a nice point of distinction between "clans" and "lineages." Within a territorial clan are small elemental descent groups whose members can spell out their common ancestry in a genealogy going back a few generations to the founder of the group. Such genealogical demonstration of membership is the traditional hallmark of a lineage. The clan in traditional usage is a unit of "putative" rather than "demonstrable" common descent: the people believe in their unitary origin but cannot trace it. In practice, membership in a clan is verified by parentage, not ancestry: one is a child of a man of the patriclan, therefore oneself a member of the clan, and therefore of the same heritage as other members.[5] Now, in certain of the

---

[3] Sahlins, *op. cit.*

[4] Bohannan, *op. cit.*, 9.

[5] Technically then, the "conical clan" is misnamed: it is a form of lineage. However, I retain here the usage originally proposed by Kirchhoff. See Paul Kirchhoff, "The Principles of Clanship in Human Society," *Davidson Journal of Anthropology*, I (1955), 1–10.

Highlands tribes, the elemental lineages are only putatively related in the clan. The traditional distinction between lineage and clan would apply here to segments of different order: lineage to the smaller groups, clan at higher levels. In other Highlands tribes, however, men of the clan do trace unbroken descent from the clan founder, a procedure that validates claims in clan lands and may be connected with acute land pressure.[6] Here, then, both lineage and so-called "clan" are genealogical groups.

The Highlands clans typically do not draw those comprehensive distinctions of genealogical seniority characteristic of conical clans. Neither persons nor lineage segments are so ranked. Nor is there a systematic set of chiefly offices, but rather local "big-men" who act as leading representatives of their subclans or clans in intergroup affairs.

Dispersed Clans

This classic form of clan [7] is the major kin unit of tribal structure in many areas. It is found on almost all continents, but especially among segmentary tribes proper.

Although a common-descent unit, matrilineal or patrilineal, the dispersed clan is quite distinct in social quality from descent groups we have been considering. For it is not a *group* but an uncoordinated *category* of people, the members of which share common status and identity, as they share ancestry, but never act as a collectivity. It would be as if all the Smiths or Joneses in America were presumed ultimately related and by that token felt special solidarity with each other, despite their dispersal over every section of the country. In the same way, members of a tribal clan are scattered in different locales and intermingled there with people of other clans. Too, they stipulate common descent but cannot demonstrate it. If they could, it might be quite marvelous, for the ancestor is sometimes held to be an animal, plant, or some other natural thing. Or the ancestor is mythically associated with such a *totem*, the clan is named from it, and emblems of it are affected by clan members as badges of identity—like the University of Michigan Wolverines or the University of Texas Longhorns. Again, despite their physical separation from each other, members of a clan form a brotherhood too close for intermarriage: clans are exogamous.

Local constellations of clansmen are usually established as lineage branches. The lineages of a clan are not ranked by descent, either internally or relative to one another: the clan is egalitarian.

Although not in itself a political group, the clan—more accurately, clanship —may have certain political functions. The local community of the tribe is likely to be a composite of lineages of different clans. But then, a single clan cross-cuts political communities, and insofar as clansmen from different places are met in economic or other cooperation this may draw their respective communities into alliance. (A tribal series of age-sets or religious or military societies similarly set across the political grain offers comparable opportunities, and may function analogously in the political sphere.)

[6] M. J. Meggitt, *The Lineage System of the Mae-Enga of New Guinea* (New York: Barnes and Noble, 1965).

[7] The unqualified "clan" or "sib" when used in anthropological discourse usually refers to this type (as above, p. 23).

The clan is not the most decentralized of major kinship structures. The tropical forests of South America may shelter small communities organized as single autonomous lineages. Among the Lapps and many Plains Indian tribes, the local group is a constellation of bilaterally related kinsmen, a *local kindred*, again without further external relations save on the level of interpersonal kinship. The To'ambaita of Malaita (Solomon Islands) exemplify autonomous kin units of still another kind, again bilateral, but in this case a proper descent group rather than a local network of kinsmen. Each district of To'ambaita is constituted as an exclusive *cognatic descent group.*

Involved in this way as the basis of territorial grouping, cognatic descent seems to specially lend itself to exclusion, if not internecine competition. For a cognatic descent community is always in theory greater than it is in fact, and some of its potential adherents are actual members of other communities. Each local group consists of descendants of a given ancestral pair. Descent is reckoned without jural emphasis on line: any combination of male and/or female links to the ancestor is legitimate and entitles one to full membership in the group. Unless, then, each group is perfectly endogamous (rarely or never the case), different corporate groups potentially overlap in personnel. Anybody, and probably just about everybody, affiliated with some particular cognatic descent unit has a father or a grandmother, or it may be a grandfather's grandmother, who is or was a member of some other group—in which therefore he is as legitimately at home as in his own. Cognatic descent cannot operate as the principle of local organization unless it is qualified in some way.[8]

The usual qualification is that one belong where one lives, and though the dispersal of one's ancestors and consanguineal kinsmen offers a choice of residences, and the options may be open to a person's descendants for generations, still one participates in the group in which he finds himself. Membership is decided by a combination of residence and descent, and the several groups thus disentangle themselves as separate local concerns. Often quite separate: the ancestors of different groups are typically not genealogically connected. Just as in effect each competes for personnel, so each stands against the world, free to maneuver in opposition to or correlation with whomever it may prove convenient.

Cognatic groups are usually not exogamous; nor are they endogamous. A cognatic descent group may be internally ranked by seniority of descent—e.g., the "houses" of Northwest Coast Indians—or it may be on that score egalitarian—e.g., To'ambaita.

Cognatic descent groups raise an issue relevant to major descent structures of many types. What exactly is the relation between the composition of a group and its ideology of descent?

---

[8] Cf. Ward H. Goodenough, "A Problem in Malayo-Polynesian Social Organization," *American Anthropologist*, LVII (1955), 71–83.

We have seen that certain "patrilineal" lineages are cognatic in actual constitution. They include descendants of female members. The group does not necessarily correspond in fact to what it is alleged to be in principle. Here as everywhere politics is an art of the possible, and, when involved in the political sphere, as the framework of a territorial section of the tribe, a patrilineal group has to make certain allowances, certain compromises. For individuals themselves are sometimes compelled to "rise above principle"— that is, to rise to the level of practicality: they have to contravene the normal rules and take up with groups in which they do not have authentic birthright. Land shortage in his own place may incline a man to settle in his wife's, and his descendants thereafter reckon his wife's patrilineage as their own. Members of a patrilineage fleeing a military disaster may find refuge among maternal kinsmen. In any set of territorial patrilineages, therefore, the *de facto* composition is likely to be cognatic. On the other hand, suppose most men of groups cognatic by ideal also put into practice a norm of patrilocal residence, remaining after marriage in their father's place. In actual membership, the cognatic group is more agnatic than certain patrilineal lineages one might name.

Clearly then, "descent" in major residential groups is a political ideology and not a mere rule of personal affiliation. It is a way of phrasing political alignments and making political differentiations. It is a charter of group rights and an expression of group solidarity. And quite beyond relating man to man within the group, the descent ideology makes connections at a higher level: it stipulates the group's relation, or lack of relation, to other groups.

The ideology of descent, then, is no simple expression of group composition or direct recognition of existing practices of personal affiliation. On the contrary, a descent dogma imposes itself on existing practices. It is quite capable of reinterpreting contradictions of membership in its own terms. Thus descendants of a woman are incorporated in her patrilineage of birth as an "accessory branch." In time, their "impure" ancestry may very well be forgotten, and the lineage genealogy is falsified to accord with patrilineal dogma. This capacity of major descent groups to override their own internal discrepancies is one very good reason for choosing to describe the tribal kinship organization from the top down. The greater groups are not the smaller writ large; it is rather the other way around. The "primary" groups and relationships are shaped by their incorporation in a larger system of a certain type.

As a political arrangement, furthermore, this larger system has its own dialectic, even as it has its own functional context. The issues transcend such domestic concerns as who associates with whom. They have to do with the continuity of the community in a tribe of communities, and with the persistence of the tribe in a world of tribes. Here too, and here decisively, are disputes joined, battles fought, alliances pledged, and cooperation effected. The principles of higher organization are forged by selective forces in play at this level. It seems more revealing to consider the segmentary lineage system, for example, in the perspective of general and external conditions (i.e., as a social instrument of inter-tribal competition) than as the working out on the tribal plane of homebred rules of lineality, a lineality that in any case is not the rule at home.

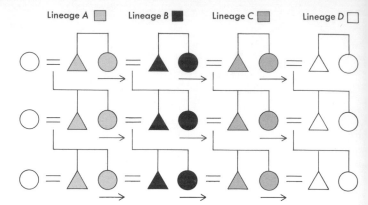

Lineage A ▢   Lineage B ◼   Lineage C ▨   Lineage D ▢

Figure 4.2. Mother's Brother's daughter marriage: flow of women between lineages.

Patterns of Marital Alliance

Marriage we like to think is the most intimate and private of human relations, however frequently it provokes the question of "Who did I marry anyhow, you or your family?" In tribal societies the issue of who really married whom is often even broader, as the lives of entire lineages are solemnly united by exchanges of their daughters. Marriage may be an arrangement of the greatest political importance, and the pattern of marriages in a tribe may amount to main lines of political alliance, complementing and in some instances even substituting for extensive descent-group relations. This holds even where the rules stipulate one should marry a particular kind of relative; for example, that a man ought marry a mother's brother's daughter. We shall discover that such a rule is not as confining of choice as it sounds, but the point of present moment is that this norm, although phrased egocentrically and in terms of individual relationships, sets up a certain "flow pattern" of women between lineages. "Mother's brother's daughter marriage" is the interpersonal expression of an interlineage alliance.[9]

The way lineages are connected by matrilateral cross-cousin marriage becomes clear when you work through a few generations of it (Fig. 4.2). I represent the intermarrying lines as patrilineal, but the result would be the same if they were matrilineal. That is, mother's brother's daughter marriage generates a one-way "direct current" of women between lineages. Lineage *B* receives wives from Lineage A and passes daughters to *C*; Lineage *C*, receiving its wives from *B*, gives women to *D*. The several lineages are linked in tandem. Each is bound by complementary relationships to two other lineages in the series, standing as "wife-giver" to one and "wife-receiver" to another. Indeed, the passage of women can very well go full circle, forming a closed marriage ring around which women circulate like discards in a game of three-handed "Pig" (and of course, there would have to be at least three lineage-sets to play the game). This "circulating connubium" is achieved if the lineage at one end of the chain supplies wives to the group at the other end (in the terms of our diagram, if the women marrying men of *A* are in fact women of *D*). Alter-

---

[9] Throughout this section I draw on structuralist understandings that have developed out of the work of Claude Lévi-Strauss—but in a highly idiosyncratic way, in no sense intended as an exposition of structuralist theory, for which purpose this discussion would be inadmissible.

nately, the marriage chain is not closed, provided arrangements exist to pump in women at one end and handle the build-up of them at the other.[10]

Alike in linking lineage to lineage in an extended series, open and closed circuits of matrilateral cross-cousin marriage potentially differ in an important political dimension. The open marriage chain uniquely lends itself to a total ranking of participating lineages. The transfer of daughters from one group to the next—perhaps against bridewealth moving the other way—may be done in token of superiority and communicate a hierarchy of status right down the line. Depending on whether giving women or receiving them is the customary mark of honor, and as you can imagine a case is easily made for either, the lineage at one end or the other of the chain stands first in a graded series of wife-dealers. (In Fig. 4.2, if wife-giving is the attribute of higher status, then Lineages A,B,C and D rank in that order; but, if wife-receiving is the noble prerogative, the rank order is reversed.) When the circuit is closed, however, a total hierarchy cannot be predicated on wife-giving or wife-receiving, for a given lineage will not be superior to all lineages outranked by the lineage it outranks. (If, in Fig. 4.2, wife-giving is reckoned superior and D supplies women to A, then D is superior to A, though A outranks B, B outranks C, and C outranks D.) But whether open and ranked, or closed and egalitarian, matrilateral cross-cousin marriage is clearly a definite strategy of lineage alliance. More than an individual preference of marriage, it is a mode of lineage coupling. Differentiating intermarrying groups into wife-givers and wife-receivers, it hitches one to another in a train of interdependent relationships.

It remains to leave the analysis of diagrams and consider the real world, where neither from the perspective of the individual nor the lineage is matrilateral cross-cousin marriage as restrictive as we have made out. "Mother's brother's daughter" does not refer to *the* mother's brother's daughter but in a classificatory scheme of things to a broad category of marriageable women. (Indeed the operative category may be broader than, but inclusive of, this set of women.) In practice, a lineage may regularly receive wives from several other lineages—all "mother's brother's daughters" of the men concerned—and likewise supply women to a number of others. The lineages are grouped in marital sets. The alliance pattern prevails among the sets. And though the proper form of marriage may be invested with special jural significance, a lineage may be free to maneuver beyond the confines of the rule and add supplementary bonds to the alliance network. That is to say (on the individual level), mother's brother's daughter marriage is not strictly obligatory or exclusively legitimate. In some cases it is merely preferred, and unions with other types of kin or with non-kin are also allowed.

(In the event of non-kin marriage, however, the new interlineage link is easily assimilated to the system forged on matrilateral cross-cousin marriage. For if an unrelated woman is acquired from another group—assume here that patrilineages are involved—then that woman's son can take another girl from her lineage in the preferred mother's brother's daughter fashion. A marriage of non-kinsmen does not then challenge the matrilateral pattern or introduce

---

[10] Cf. Edmund R. Leach, "Structural Implications of Matrilateral Cross Cousin Marriage," *Journal of the Royal Anthropological Institute*, LXXXI (1951), 23–55.

another principle of alliance: it merely expands wife-giving and wife-receiving sets, which is to say, extends the range of the matrilateral chain.)[11]

Different norms of cross-cousin marriage develop different configurations of interlineage alliance. Where matrilateral cross-cousin marriage sets in motion a direct current of women between lineages, the patrilateral form (father's sister's daughter marriage) establishes an alternating current. In one generation women are transferred in one direction; in the next generation the flow is reversed (Fig. 4.3). A given lineage looks first one way for women, then

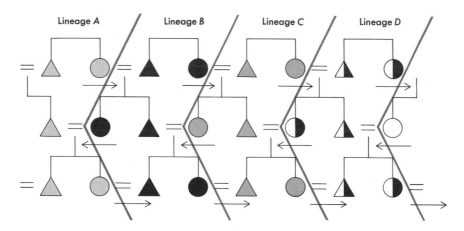

Figure 4.3. Patrilateral cross-cousin marriage: flow of women between lineages (patrilineal).

another. In the senior generation of Fig. 4.3, Lineage B receives wives from Lineage A and passes daughters to Lineage C; but in the succeeding generation, B supplies daughters to A and gets wives from C; the third round then repeats the first. (Again, in practice marital sets rather than single lineages would normally be involved.)

Like matrilateral cross-cousin marriage, the patrilateral variety composes a chain of interlinked lineages. Too, the chain may be closed to form a marriage circuit. But the relationship of intermarrying groups, the form of linkage, is

---

[11] There is no structural difference between obligatory matrilateral cross-cousin marriage and preferred matrilateral cross-cousin marriage with non-kin marriage allowed. That is, the character of the alliance network is the same in either event. The difference is that one (obligatory) is a static, and the other (preferred) a dynamic, version of this structure. *Mutatis mutandis*, the same holds for all other types of cross-cousin marriage: the preferred-with-non-kin-allowed is a dynamic form of the obligatory. Conceivably, the structural status-quo is maintained even if unions with kinsmen other than the proper cross-cousin are allowed, so long as the cross-cousin rule is jurally emphasized: other marriages can be assimilated to the proper cross-cousin marriage, and in the next generation the system picks up on standard course. Suppose the rule is matrilateral cross-cousin marriage and I marry a patrilateral cross-cousin. True, it disrupts the system, but only temporarily and only in one sector. My son, marrying his mother's brother's daughter, gets a woman from the same lineage as I did. What has happened is that that lineage and my own have merely reversed their previous wife-giving and wife-receiving relation.

here quite distinct. Intermarrying groups are not functionally differentiated into suppliers of women and wife-receivers, and a particular lineage is not connected on one side with a group from which it regularly gets women and on the other side a group to whom it customarily gives women. In a pattern of delayed exchange, each lineage instead maintains *reciprocal* relations with its marriage-partners on both sides. Where the system is patrilineal, a lineage returns on the next round the daughters of women received from partner-lineages on the preceding round. Consistently canceling such invidious distinctions as might be drawn from giving women or receiving them, this reciprocity makes it difficult to utilize the transfer of women for interlineage ranking. If anything, patrilateral marriage seems designed to perpetuate the dignity and equality of all concerned, so long as each group is careful to reciprocate in kind the charming favors it had latterly received.

Patrilateral and matrilateral cross-cousin marriage are not as fashionable in the tribal world as they are in anthropological discussions of it. Bilateral cross-cousin marriage—that is, preferred or obligatory unions with cross-cousins of any sort, without discrimination between matrilateral and patrilateral types—is more popular.[12] In most tribes of this persuasion no distinction is indeed drawn between matrilateral and patrilateral cross-cousins: they are joined in a single classificatory category ("cross-cousin").

Bilateral cross-cousin marriage is a most adaptable way of making relatives out of lineages. Any marriage of cross-cousins unites members of different lineages, whatever the permutation of patrilineal or matrilineal descent and patrilateral or matrilateral cousin. The student might wish to work this out for himself. Probably in making his genealogies he will assume that three lineages are involved (e.g., ego's own patrilineage, his mother's, and his father's sister's husband's), and thus discover that the bilateral marriage rule opens to ego's lineage the possibility of contracting with either of the other two. Seemingly, alliances are not as constrained as under a unilateral rule. And were one to assume more lineages in the system, and to allow classificatory cross-cousin marriage, the opportunities for marital maneuver would seem even greater.

A nice theory could be spun from this apparent versatility, and perhaps an explanation of the popularity of bilateral cross-cousin marriage: that it is a system of nuptial *Realpolitik*. In allowing calculated dispositions of their sons and daughters, cross-cousin marriage seems to allow lineages the greatest freedom of response to practical considerations. The elders can weigh the comparative economic and political merits of combining with this group or that. Yet no marriage need have the *look* of expediency. It follows the cross-cousin norm, and it can usually be taken as a reinforcement of some previous union between the groups concerned. In the latter event, the reaffirmation of the kinship of lineages would especially permit the people to conceal what is

---

[12] I judge from a very rough analysis of approximately 225 tribal level societies with unilateral descent tabulated by Professor Murdock that about 14 per cent show a bias toward matrilateral cross-cousin marriage, 5 per cent toward patrilateral, and 28 per cent toward bilateral. Many cases of matrilateral and patrilateral, however, only prefer the one while allowing the other. Superficially these cases resemble bilateral cross-cousin marriage. See George P. Murdock, "World Ethnographic Sample," *American Anthropologist*, 1957, LIX, 664–687.

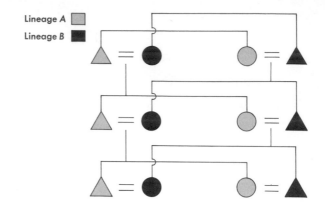

Figure 4.4. Simple model of "sister exchange."

Lineage A ▢
Lineage B ▪

fundamentally a calculated move by a grand display of that maudlin sentimentality in which they are wont to indulge on all such occasions.

But the alliance options of cross-cousin marriage, even classificatory cross-cousin marriage, are not in fact unlimited, nor will the ensuing lines of alliance merely demonstrate the vectors of opportunistic choice. There is always a *dual organization* evident in the alliance formations: selection of mates from certain groups is prohibited, while marriages with certain other groups are allowed.

Indeed, suppose instead of the three lineages diagramed by our hypothetical student, two lineages entered into a long-term agreement to reciprocally exchange their daughters. Phrased another way, they insist upon *sister-exchange*, that a man give his own (or lineage) sister in return for the sister given him as wife by a member of the other group. Here we have the most inbred system of alliance conceivable: two lineages endlessly combining and recombining through reciprocal transfers of their womenfolk. But notice (Fig. 4.4) what it entails in terms of marriage choice: bilateral cross-cousin marriage. That is truly the apposite term, for a man's wife is simultaneously related to him as father's sister's and mother's brother's daughter. And what would be the shape of the tribal alliance network? It is fractioned into small endogamous cliques, each composed of a pair of exogamous groups that, as it were, subsist on each other and are cut off, save perhaps for remote bonds of clanship, from like pairs elsewhere. Certain Amazonian tribes display just this form of dual organization, with each village a union of two intermarrying halves.[13]

But even if the direct exchange of women is not enjoined and many lineages widely dispersed are embraced in the marriage scheme, and unions with remote classificatory cross-cousins are perfectly acceptable, even then the interlineage alliances are not *ad hoc*. A structure exists that transcends expediency and circumscribes it: in principle, the self-same dualism. I can most briefly explain by referring to Fig. 4.5, adding just this note, that in the classificatory terminology usually associated with cross-cousin marriage, cross-cousins of my own cross-cousins are my "brothers" and "sisters." In that event, the daughters of only some of the lineages figured are marriageable, as far as I am concerned, and only some lineages may be thus allied with my own. The girl g, for example, is my potential wife. As witnessed by the marriages of girls of Lineage D

---

[13] The two halves of the village, however, are usually not constituted as single lineages but as exogamous *moieties* composed of several clan-sections each, a qualification that bears on the ensuing discussion. The social self-sufficiency involved may help explain an unusual capacity of South American tribalism, that the "tribe" is sometimes a single village, and that village, the tribe.

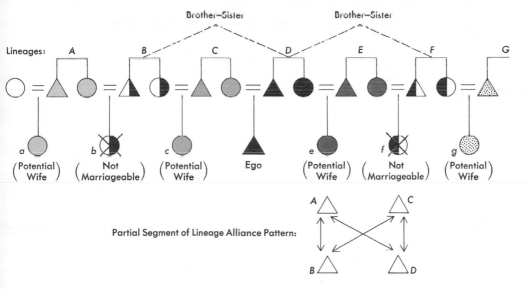

Figure 4.5. *Alliance pattern of bilateral cross-cousin marriage (own and classificatory).*

with E and of E with F, the people of D and F are "brother" and "sister," both cross-cousins of E. Therefore, g's mother (an F) is "sister" to my father (a D); hence, g is a "father's sister's daughter" (cross-cousin). By a similar exegesis, I can take a wife from Lineage A, and of course from my cross-cousins of Lineages C and F. I cannot, however, marry f, a cross-cousin of my cross-cousin and thus a "sister," nor likewise the girl b. It follows that there is a set of lineages, B, F, etc., into which my lineage does not marry— half the lineages of the network, including my own; and another series, Lineages A, C, E, G, etc., into which we people of D can marry—that is, the other half of the network.

In other words, here is exactly the dual organization of sister-exchange, only now opposing two extended sets of dispersed lineages. A given lineage cannot marry within its moiety, although it may contract with any of the opposite moiety. Lineages of its own set are in some sense "own people." The opposing moiety is "the others"—and *Realpolitik* is confined to dealings with them. On one plane or another, this duality is an inescapable condition of bilateral cross-cousin marriage. The system is further liberalized, made freely opportunistic, only by breaking that rule (which some people who insist on it in theory are known regularly to do).

We see that in its several varieties, cross-cousin marriage entails a comparatively structured tribal universe, of dualism, or of one or another kind of marriage chain. When cousin marriage is prohibited, a course also adopted by numerous peoples, the alliance network becomes at once more generalized and more intricate. This complexity is introduced by simple rules; for example, a flat injunction on marriage between all cousins within a certain degree (usually second or third cousins), or a general prohibition of marriage with any relative. It thus becomes difficult or impossible for each generation to duplicate the alliances of the last. Any given family continuously develops new affinal connections, and over the long term maintains a broad if changing field of consanguineal kin. If, in addition, regional endogamy is customary, the people are joined in a great web of interlocking and overlapping kin relationships. These marital arrangements seem most useful to a system of cognatic descent groups or a local-kindred organization. The extended network of bilateral relations can be mobilized to build up local communities, and to facilitate alliances with other groups. But rules similar to the injunction on cousin marriage are also imposed in certain lineage systems—if only to depreciate the solidarities of marriage in favor of those of lineage!

Marriage is one principle of political allegiance, lineage another. They may complement each other, but where lineage relations prevail between local groups—as in segmentary lineage systems—they may seriously compete. What side do you take when your relatives by marriage dispute with your relatives by lineage? Phrased on a higher level, a group soon discovers its obligations toward affinal kinsmen conflict with its duties toward brother lineages. The contradiction is endemic in lineage systems, but it can be minimized by a "prohibition of parallel marriage"; that is, a bar on repeated unions between the same lineages. It is forbidden a man to take a wife from any group (it may be a lineage, subclan, or clan) into which a member of his own group has recently married—and of course he cannot marry within his own group. The rule may be formulated as a broad range of personal tabus, prescribing marriage with a close cognate, with a member of one's mother's patrilineage, with a member of one's father's mother's lineage, with a daughter of any woman of one's own patrilineage, etc. Precluding duplication of existing inter-lineage ties, these prohibitions have the effect of extending marital connections to the greatest possible number of outside groups.

On one hand, the injunction on parallel marriage seems a strategy of maximum alliance. Where affinal relatives are relied upon economically, the rule will indeed create a wide field of exchange partners. On the other hand, it may put marriage at a *political* discount, for if the alliances of a given lineage are widely spread, they are also spread thin. Each lineage is bound to another by only a single strand. Each transaction in women is nonreciprocal and discontinuous. As a mode of alliance, this is the next thing to lineage endogamy, which is a program of socialism in one country. Rather than maximum alliance, it approaches maximum exclusiveness. Nonparallel marriage would be consistent with a tribal organization in which autonomous unilineal groups stand counterposed to each other in a state of sustained argument. Thus it is found among the Dobuans of Melanesia, whose matrilineal clan-section villages live in dread of sorcery from all directions, and among the Mae Enga, who like many New Guinea Highlanders are content to "fight the people we marry" (and vice versa). Nonparallel marriage lends itself to a local consensus of belligerence toward everyone else. In case of dispute with another lineage, at best only one of the local families, directly connected by marriage with that group, might have reservations about the propriety of finishing them off.

The Enga suggest another context of nonparallel marriage, one mentioned before and perhaps best seen among the Nuer of the Eastern Sudan: a segmentary lineage system. Here again the diffusion of marital ties can rob them of political efficacy, and thus give full play to the superstructure of lineage relations. Spread judiciously among a number of outside groups, the marital connections of any particular lineage and unable to compete with its external lineage connections as a basis of higher political collaboration.

Whether it consolidates the local line (Dobu) or the lineage superstructure (Nuer), the prohibition of parallel marriage has the same general effect: discounting the marriage principle, it capitalizes the lineage principle to the point of political monopoly.[14]

Families and
Familial Relationships

The ideal household in many tribes includes two or more married couples and their children. This *extended family* is apparently more often customary than an independent *nuclear family* (i.e., the elemental unit of husband, wife, and their offspring).[15]

The preference may be rooted in circumstances of production. An extended family spreads the economic risks, taking up the slack of poor or incapacitated producers. More important, its comparatively large manpower pool equips it for diversified and extensive activities, as often are involved in a neolithic economy. It is able to handle simultaneously a complex of tasks: herding, various gardening procedures, hunting, gathering, not to mention babysitting and other domestic crafts (such as making pottery). An extended family may prove especially useful during labor "choke periods," when many hands are needed for clearing forest, harvesting, or pasturing livestock. Not the least of its virtues, an extended family can be deployed over a wide area, to exploit different local opportunities: some family members can be detached for long periods in care of distant gardens or grazing herds while others are "just working around the house." In these several economic aspects, an extended family would appear to have the advantage over smaller nuclear groups.

The thesis implied, that the extended family is a structural adaptation to an economic complication is easily elaborated. For example, some centralization is also implied—a headman to schedule and allocate tasks—so if the family is "a little chiefdom within the chiefdom," it is no mere domestic conceit. But production alone does not a family make, and no amount of allusion to this function suffices to resolve the details of family organization. The family is infixed in a larger social system, to the support of which it contributes more than material wherewithal. The family in its everyday activities rehearses kinds of behavior and attitudes necessary to the running of the larger system. In the measure of that function, the family order is molded by the tribal order, and even in its most intimate relationships bears the impress of society at large.

Paradoxically, the intrinsic weakness of the tribal order is at issue. Lacking coercive means, the superstructure is incapable of actively imposing itself upon the domestic infrastructure. The norms and sentiments of collective life must

---

[14] Cf. Jack and Esther Goody, "Cross-cousin Marriage in Northern Ghana," *Man*, new series I (1966), 343–355.

[15] I judge (again, by rough analysis) from Murdock's "World Ethnographic Sample" that extended families are the norm in about 56 per cent of tribal societies. In many of the remaining 44 per cent, polygyny (thus, "polygynous extended families") is the ideal.

be absorbed instead in the tissues of family life. The family, then, takes the imprint of the polity, the smaller group the form of the larger, so that from top to bottom the same principles are in play. Thus harmonized with the larger organization of society, the family sees in the former the image of its own existence, as well as the course of its own development. The gains from this economizing of tribal structure are banked in the higher, political levels of the system, which are thereby empowered not with coercive force but with those natural understandings and that compliance in the scheme of things that children ingest with their mother's milk.

To refer the "little chiefdom within the chiefdom" to production is therefore not enough. The little chiefdom is the greater chiefdom transposed to the household level. Polynesian family relationships, for example, are systematically differentiated by rank to an extent far beyond functional demands of a domestic economy. The family is thoroughly assimilated to the conical clan in which it is embedded. Like the great chief in his domain, the father is in his own house a sacred figure, a man of superior *mana*, his possessions, even his food, guarded by tabus against defilement by lesser familial kinsmen. Polynesians know innately how to honor the chief, for chieftainship begins at home: the chief's due is no more than elaborate filial respect.[16] In the same vein, the oldest child of the house commands ritual deference from his younger siblings. But then, primogeniture holds in the family as in the clan, and the gradations of genealogical seniority it implies hold as well, affecting the way people address each other, customs of standing and sitting in another's presence, and a thousand other minutiae of domestic intercourse. The physical structure of the house is itself symbolically accommodated to clan organization. Divided into socially "higher" and "lower" spaces, it makes a perfect exoskeleton for the differentiated family organism. In all family activities— eating, sleeping, or just talking—the men of the family spatially dispose themselves in the house according to their seniority. Clearly, to be raised in such an atmosphere can only be, as far as Polynesian society is concerned, "a proper up-bringing."

Now let us put the general problem of extended families in this light. Whatever its economic advantages, the extended family has the political advantage of comprising a descent group in miniature. Consider the *patrilocal extended family*: a patriarch, his wife, his married sons with their wives and children, and perhaps some unmarried daughters of the senior couple (Fig. 4.6). Without further detail, it is already clear that this family selectively accents certain patterns of relationship: the solidarity of paternal kinsmen, the subordination of junior-generation paternal kinsmen to senior, the detachment of women from their natal groups for procreation of their husbands' heirs. This is exactly the stuff lineages are made of, the very principles ("jural rules") of the patrilineal lineage. A family so constituted makes a domestic virtue of a political conception. Such is its contribution to the continuity of that conception. One concludes that a society of patrilineal lineages is predisposed to patrilocal extended families, whatever the economy.

The patrilocal extended family is generated by a rule of patrilocal marital residence: newlyweds join the husband's natal house. Other norms of resi-

---

[16] Reciprocally, the great chief is metaphorically "father to the people," which reinforces this generalization of rank etiquette.

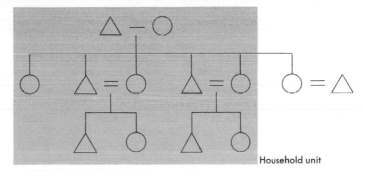

Figure 4.6. Patrilocal extended family.

Household unit

dence are used to develop other family forms. The following paragraphs consider briefly some of the main varieties of family structure and residence rule found in tribes, as well as the social contexts with which these domestic arrangements seem most consistent.[17]

The polygynous family of a man, his several wives, and their offspring is like the patrilocal extended family, a patrilineage in microcosm: a patriarch surrounded by coteries of dependents and descendants. The man's sons, however, ordinarily break away upon marriage and establish independent households (neolocal residence), although these may be near their father's home. The differences between this and the patrilocal family system may reflect subtle differences in the enclaving lineage system. The full patrilocal family implies collateral solidarity among agnates, the brother-brother bond, as well as lineal, father-son solidarity. The polygynous family emphasizes the latter only. The polygynous family suggests then a more fissiparous lineage, with some proneness to segment at low levels.

Matrilocal marital residence puts the newly married couple in the wife's natal house. The *matrilocal extended family* thus formed is a mirror image of the patrilocal, and implies the opposite descent-group matrix, matrilineal lineages. Matrilocality arranges the females of a matriline—the members that provide group continuity—in stable association. On the other hand, avunculocal residence—the couple joining the house of the husband's mother's brother—also confers matrilineal benefits. It concentrates the adult males of a matriline (Fig. 4.7). The *avunculocal extended family*, however, is not so common as the matrilocal. It seems to be associated with the transmission of special prerogatives, chieftainships notably, between males of a matriline; hence, it is argued, avunculocality is a practice of the more developed matrilineal systems.

In what is called "bilocal residence," a married couple has the option of joining the husband's or the wife's people. The choice taken depends on various relative advantages, such as the availability of land in the two homesteads. An extended family constructed on this basis—a *bilocal extended family*—might include married sons and/or married daughters of the senior couple. In its own form, the family suggests a larger bilateral emphasis; e.g., cognatic descent groups or local kindreds. The measure of option in residence and family composition is further consistent with the openness of bilateral groups, which tolerate considerable flexibility in affiliation. Neolocal residence

---

[17] One cannot insist on the correspondence between family and higher-level structures, for there is of course a possibility of independent variation and ethnography will (as always) put exceptions to the rule of consistency.

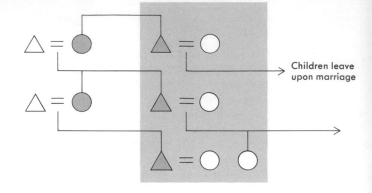

*Figure 4.7. The avuncu-
local extended family.*

Children leave
upon marriage

and nuclear family autonomy, however, are in this respect equally suited to a non-lineage superstructure.

Family relationships are subject to the greater system in detail as well as in general, in specific content as well as in broad outline. Matrilineal and patrilineal descent, or more precisely, matrilineal and patrilineal lineages, evoke contrasts in the relationship between husbands and wives, for example, or between brothers and sisters. Again I speak only of tendencies. In specific cases the constraints of a mode of descent may be buried and covered over, proved no match for countervailing circumstances.

Still the chances are that marriage is more stable in a patrilineal order, and the divorce rate higher in a matrilineal. The difference arises from the different roles women play in maintaining group continuity. A woman bears the children of her husband's patrilineage, but of her own matrilineage. The fate of a patrilineage hinges on the control men gain over their wives and their wives' productivity. Marriage must then challenge a woman's connections to her natal kinsmen and in some sense capture her for her husband's. It has been observed of certain African societies that bride prices tend to be more substantial in the patrilineal tribes than in those with matrilineal or double descent. But then the rights in women conveyed by marriage are more substantial in strong patrilineal systems. The husband claims not merely wifely services but the woman as child-bearer, her progeny—whoever in fact may sire them. The children belong to him and his, primarily to him but residually to his lineage, who in event of his demise may perpetuate the group's interest by supplying another husband (e.g., the deceased man's brother). As a matter of lineage persistence, a marriage can outlast the particular partners to it. This import of marriage to the lineage as a corporation is manifest more particularly in the durability of husband-wife relations, and in a complementary dilution of a married woman's relations to her brother—standing for her lineage of birth.

Matrilineal descent imposes exactly opposite demands. It is legitimate to continue to take the man's point of view here, for even in matrilineages men usually dominate corporate affairs and fill lineage offices. But a man's heirs are his sister's children, not his own; and lineage continuity rests with his control of his sister and her offspring, not his wife and hers. What is conveyed to a husband in patrilineal marriage cannot be conveyed in matrilineal marriage. Men, on the contrary, retain strong interests in their sisters even as against their wives, while women are bound to their brothers as against their husbands. Although matrilocality may be the rule, a husband in taking up with his wife's people does not sever attachments to his mother's and sister's home

—where he can usually find refuge from a nagging wife and her cabal of domineering kinswomen. Other things being equal, husband-wife relations are likely to be more brittle than in a patrilineal order, and brother-sister relations firmer.

The mode of descent may also condition the kinship of father and son, and of maternal uncle and nephew. In a patrilineal system, the father-son relation is an unequal one, demanding of the latter due regard and submission. (At the same time, however, the son is his father's heir, and this double role of subordinate and successor is not without its possibilities of conflict.) As for the mother's brother-sister's son relationship, Fijians call it "heavy," and in explanation echo certain anthropologists: maternal uncle and nephew compose a direct consanguineal link between two different paternal lines. Here are two males of distinct lineage who are yet "blood" kinsmen. His sister's son is a man's "blood" in his sister's husband's group, the personal embodiment of the alliance broached by his sister's marriage. In Fijian society and many others, this alliance between lineages is epitomized in the behavior expected between mother's brother and sister's son—that is, in an institutionalized *avunculate*. Unlike the dominance of father over son, *mutual* regard and esteem (if not special affection) are enjoined on maternal uncle and nephew. Furthermore, powerful obligations of gift-giving or economic aid attach to the relationship, sometimes to the distinct advantage of the nephew—who in Fiji, for example, is accorded exaggerated respect and permitted free access to his uncle's goods. The interlineage connection is symbolized in a kind of formal "friendship," a ritualized regard, between maternal uncle and nephew.

All this is likely to be inverted in matrilineal societies. Here the mother's brother is the lineage authority, and the sister's son submissive to his discipline; whereas, the father-child dyad is the interlineage alliance, imbued with mutuality and affection—and those small parental favors made "extras" by their transmission outside the framework of matrilineal obligations.

Interpersonal
Kinship Patterns

We have moved from the big pattern to the small, from the tribal to the familial. Last comes the individual and his social world. Rest assured he has not been least in the esteem of our anthropologists. If anything he is the main preoccupation, in traditional analyses the central subject from whose vantage the entire organization is perceived, the all-purpose universal "ego," a full member of every tribe from the Arapaho to the Zuni, sitting there at the navel of a kinship diagram that represents the way the world is ordered for him, and so for us, "the kinship system" of the people.

Nevertheless, a warning: This pattern of relationships is not "the kinship system" but the way it is presented to an individual, the shadow it casts before. It is an idiom by which "the system" intrudes upon people's lives, to animate them in ways consistent with its own functioning. Our identification with "the individual" can become an undue concern, and of "the kinship system" with its personal aspect an unmerited conceit, a projection perhaps from our own conviction of the supreme importance of the individual and our propensity to see things by his lights—paradoxically by raising him to the level of a collective representation and thus destroying his individuality. At least it may be misleading. The pattern of kin relationships represents those discriminations in classification and behavior made among people as a result of their arrangement by the rules and modes of tribal structure. Of course it is important; on the level of interpersonal discourse, all important. But it is contingent, a refraction of greater social institutions, and in the final analysis, which is where it properly belongs, rather a worm's-eye view of "the system."

This polemic delivered, I should like to take up in detail one such pattern of kinship. But first, an extended digression, by way of preparing you for some shocks—and for some deficiencies in the analysis. We have to deal here with the way a person's relatives are classified, are put into certain nominal categories, which presumably says something about the way they are treated. The classifications tribesmen make are often quite curious to us. They may group within the same *kinship* type people of very disparate *genealogical* type, people we would never dream of classing together. But, one supposes, in the light of *their* institutions—the local mode of descent, for instance, or the form of residence or norm of marriage—the classification will make sense.

From here out (and perhaps even before) arguments ensue among anthropologists about how to proceed from social practice to kinship terminology. The prevailing view is that existing institutions will align one's relatives in broad categories, such as "marriageable," "non-marriageable," "of my mother's patrilineage," "of my father's local group," and the like. Kinsmen differently placed in my genealogy may nevertheless share the same status relative to myself. Therefore, they are conceived and labeled alike, as kinsmen of one kind.[18]

Consider, for instance, the classifications of the accompanying diagram (Fig. 4.8), a small portion of a so-called *Crow* terminology. The Roman numerals stand for kinship categories; thus, my father, father's sister's son, and father's sister's daughter's son are in custom the same type of kinsman (II). Now from our point of view here is some very peculiar practice. Certain relatives of my own and my children's generation are related to me as is my father, referred to by the same term. Then, my own children and my brother's are classed with my mother's brother's (VII), which for us would make all the nonsense of calling a certain cousin "son." Yet it might be eminently sensible to the people concerned, supposing they were arranged in matrilineal groups. Then indeed all the men in Category II have a similar status, "man of my father's lineage"; similarly all III's are "woman of my father's lineage." My own and my mother's brother's children again are comparably positioned in a matrilineal order—*viz.*, as children of my lineage, "of my lineage" but not in it. Hence the traditional interpretation of Crow terminology: that it reflects "strong" corporate matrilineages, so important in everyday life that the generation-status of certain collateral relatives is less material to the way I consider them than their lineage status.

Sensible as it seems, there are many reasons to fault this perspective, even apart from the particular suspicion that "strong corporate matrilineages" is

---

[18] As we shall see, the arguments begin when certain genealogically distant members of a given kinship category are discovered not to have the institutional status by which the category presumably was defined.

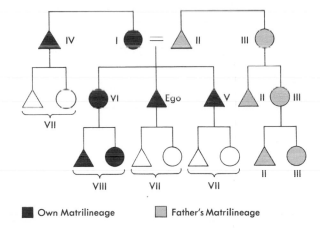

Figure 4.8. Section of a Crow terminology.

■ Own Matrilineage   ▦ Father's Matrilineage

something of a tautological extrapolation from strong matrilineal kin-reckoning. Also, in this particular case the adequacy of lineage affiliation as a comprehensive explanation of Crow categories has been seriously challenged on grounds that, when applied to more distant relatives than those depicted, category terms do not necessarily correspond to lineage-statuses.[19] This is recent criticism. That the kinship classifications of a particular tribe may be out of joint with current social practices has been known from the beginning of kinship studies. Kinship terminology may have a life of its own, longer than the institutions which presumably gave rise to it. Moreover, social practices implying contradictory kinship classifications may co-exist in the same tribe. It is therefore frequently difficult to correlate terminology with sociology —which leads some anthropologists into speculative reconstructions of social history, and others to despair of sociological "explanations."

Before we despair, I shall describe more fully one well known kinship pattern and suggest some of the ways it can be "explained"—i.e., some of the possible co-existing institutions. After that, we can reasonably despair.

Figure 4.9 is an actual ethnographic example, complete with native terms. It is of the general type called *Iroquois* or *bifurcate-merging*, and of the particular subtype *Dravidian*. The version I present here is the Fijian.[20] The diagram includes the three central generations of the terminology of reference; that is, the way people allude to various kinsmen, which may differ from the way they address them.

In the Fijian classification, father and father's brother are in the same kinship category (I, *tamaqu*), as is mother's sister's husband. It can be assumed that members of the same general category are generally alike in their behavior toward ego, and that he behaves similarly toward all of them; but in some contexts discriminations are made, as, e.g., between "own" father and his brothers. Father's older and younger brothers are indeed distinguished as "great father" and "little father," respectively. Of the other relatives in this senior generation, mother, mother's sister, and father's brother's wife are classed together (II, *tinaqu*), and these ladies are distinguished from father's

[19] Floyd Lounsbury, "A Formal Account of the Crow- and Omaha-Type Kinship Terminologies," in Ward H. Goodenough, ed., *Explorations in Cultural Anthropology: Essays in Honor of George Peter Murdock* (New York: McGraw-Hill, 1964), pp. 351–393.

[20] Students who have read Elman Service's *The Hunters* in this Series will find there a general discussion of a bifurcate-merging pattern. The Fijian terminology figured here I collected in Moala Island of that group.

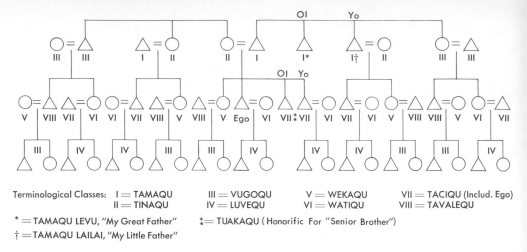

Terminological Classes: I = TAMAQU   III = VUGOQU   V = WEKAQU   VII = TACIQU (Includ. Ego)
                         II = TINAQU   IV = LUVEQU   VI = WATIQU   VIII = TAVALEQU

* = TAMAQU LEVU, "My Great Father"   ⁎= TUAKAQU (Honorific For "Senior Brother")
† = TAMAQU LAILAI, "My Little Father"

Figure 4.9. Fijian kinship terminology.

sister and mother's brother's wife (III, *vugoqu*). The latter two are in a class
with mother's brother and father's sister's husband. Terminology in my own
generation may be described by these rules: (1) children of a I (*tamaqu*,
"father")[21] and a II (*tinaqu*, "mother") are if males VII, (*taciqu*, "brothers")
and if females V (*wekaqu*, "sisters"), with the exception that one's senior
brother (*tuakaqu*) is further differentiated from the II class; and (2) children
of III's (*vugoqu*, the "mother's brother-father's sister" class) are if males VIII
("male cross-cousins," *tavalequ*) and if females VI (*watiqu*), to which last
class also belongs my wife. Put another way, siblings and parallel cousins of
the same sex are classed together and differentiated from cross-cousins of that
sex. In the succeeding generation, children of a VII ("brother") and a VI
("female cross-cousin," "wife"), including my own children, are alike IV
(*luvequ*, "children"); whereas, children of a V (*wekaqu*, "sister") and VIII
(*tavalequ*, "male cross-cousin") are in a different category, III (*vugoqu*)—the
same one as my mother's brother and father's sister. In other words, my children and those of my brothers, male parallel cousins and female cross-cousins
are classed together but distinguished from the category embracing children
of my sisters, female parallel cousins and male cross-cousins. The latter children are classed with my maternal uncle and paternal aunt.

What does it all mean? Conceivably a number of things: a variety of
institutional arrangements would in whole or in part resolve the classifications
of this terminology; that is to say, would correlate and oppose my kinsmen in
exactly the same ways. But there is a difference in the power of different institutional explanations. Some are comprehensive: the social practice adduced
(e.g., cross-cousin marriage) may generate a common status for all genealogical
types represented in a kinship category, thus accounting for the category and
indeed a series of necessarily related categories. Others are not comprehensive
but are in some degree incomplete: they "make sense" only of the inclusion

---

21 In translating the term for a Fijian category such as *tamaqu* by the English term for
the nearest relative of that category, "father," I grievously violate current scruples, for thus
prejudging the "meaning" (or "primary meaning") of the Fijian category infiltrates a whole
theory of how terms are developed and genealogically "extended." But it is easier to follow,
and opinions being divided as they are, I will bear the strictures of colleagues that I might
earn the gratitude of students—I hope without terribly misleading them.

of certain near kinsmen within the category. The latter explanations open a Pandora's box of theoretical miseries, most of the issues currently in debate— What do kinship terms "mean"? Is it legitimate to discriminate "primary" and "secondary" meanings of a given term? If so, how are terms extended from primary to secondary referents? [22] I don't know the answers. So I offer the student the rare privilege (in an introductory text) of playing humanity to my Pandora.

What social arrangements, then, would generate the terminological distinctions of Fig. 4.9?

Allow me first to simplify by taking for granted that sex and generation standing are usually differentiated, so that a kin category is specific to members of one sex and one generation level. Interest attaches to the exceptions, especially the class III (*vugoqu*), about which more presently, and the distinctions of relative age among ego's own brothers and father's brothers. These distinctions of relative age suggest a hierarchy by birth order among paternal kinsmen, thus immediately an internally ranked patrilocal extended family. That the Fijians do have. Consider also the translations, "my great father" for father's older brother, and "my little father" for father's younger brother. (Indeed, in address father is "*Ratu*," which roughly is "noble," and father's senior brother, "*Ratu Levu*," "great noble.") The seniority distinctions of a conical clan are conjured up. And that too lurks in the Fijian background. Rank by descent in fact pervades relations of near kinsmen far more than can be illustrated here.

Might patrilineal descent groups be otherwise relevant to the conceptions of this terminology? Note that father and father's brother are classed together (I) and differentiated from mother's brother (III). Given a rule of patrilineal affiliation, my father and his brother do share an important status: they are senior men of the same group (which is also my own), and they differ in respect of lineage from mother's brother. The identification of their wives (FaBrWi = Mo) is consistent and perhaps derivative. Also, like my father and his brother, mother and mother's sister share lineage status and in this they differ from father's sister. Hence the comparable equations, Mo = MoSi FaSi, and MoSiHu = Fa. That opposition, repeated throughout, between own- and parallel-relatives on one side, and cross relatives on the other, is established at least in this set of senior-generation kinsmen.

Furthermore, the categorical distinctions in my own generation are then logically derivative. It is consistent that the children of my parents and my parents' parallel siblings (that is, of my "mothers" and "fathers") are classed together and differentiated from my mother's brother's and father's sister's children (my "cross-cousins"). Without further assumptions, the distinctions appearing in terms applied to my own, my siblings', and my parallel cousins' children also follow. We are "brothers" and "sisters," and the children of

---

[22] It is sometimes supposed that the insufficiency of certain institutional explanations of kin categories also calls into question the validity of any such sociological explanation. The most sophisticated semantic analyses, however, have not put at issue the sociological determination of kinship so much as the kind of social explanation that would be appropriate.

See Floyd Lounsbury, "A Formal Account of the Crow- and Omaha-Type Kinship Terminologies," and "Another View of Trobriand Kin Categories," in E. A. Hammel, ed., *Formal Semantic Analysis*, Special Publication, *American Anthropologist*, LXVII (1965), No. 5, Part 2, 142–185.

brothers are classed together and distinguished from children of sisters. Many of the main differentiations and mergers throughout the three generations can thus be logically predicated from patrilineal descent. The only *caveat* is that tribesmen are under no obligation to apply the logic. Many peoples make the same classifications the Fijians do in the senior (parental) generation, followed by "Hawaiian" terminology in ego's generation; i.e., all cousins, parallel and cross, are alike "brothers" and "sisters."

In the above particulars, the Fijian kinship scheme is consistent with patrilineal descent; and as I say, Fijians are socially biased that way. But patrilineal descent is not unique in its capacity to generate these distinctions. "Patrilocal" could be substituted for "patrilineal" throughout the preceding analysis, and "local group," then, for "lineage," without damage (or further damage) to the logic. The same is true of "matrilineal" and "matrilocal"! They would as well yield the specified classifications. But then, Fijian terminology is not unique either. It is one of a broad class of similar schemes. In the respects at issue, this type of terminology is harmonious with a variety of common modes of group formation.

We neglected something. It is understandable in the context of patrilineal descent why mother should be classed with her sister as opposed to father's sister, and father with his brother as opposed to mother's brother. But why the correlation of maternal uncle and paternal aunt in the same category, *vugoqu* (III), along with such relatives as sister's son? Something can be said as well about this classification by reference to patrilineal descent, but in an incomplete way, as it pertains to these particular members of the category. In the Fijian view, mother's brother, father's sister, and sister's son play similar and critical roles as consanguineal points of connection between ego's and affinally related patrilines, as people on (or through) whom devolves the alliance-function of marriage. They are the flying buttresses of ego's line. I think it fair to say that these kinsmen, especially own mother's brother and sister's son, are "primary" members of the category *vugoqu*. Notice too that the relation between mother's brother and sister's son is "self-reciprocal": you are related to your mother's brother as he is to you, as if you were also "uncle" to your "uncle"—and likewise in Fijian custom father's sister and her brother's son are *vugoqu* to each other. In other words, here is just that mutuality we suggested would occur in those personal relationships that carry lineage alliances; but notably, in a patrilineal order, between mother's brother and sister's son.

Still it is obvious that mother's brother and father's sister operate differently as kinsmen of alliance, and their common categorization is somewhat puzzling. Functionally, the maternal uncle-nephew relation is more strategic, as here are two consanguineally-connected men of different patrilines. On the other hand, the role of the father's sister resembles that of a sister in interlineage alliance: a female of my own line through whom liaison is effected. Here Fijian terminology of address rescues us. Maternal uncle and paternal aunt are not altogether similar in Fijian kinship estimations. They are often distinguished in address if not in reference. And, on the other hand, father's sister *is* partially identified with sister. *Gane* is an alternate term of reference for "sister" (man speaking, *ganequ* = "my sister"), and *ganei* is a common term of address for "father's sister" (usually glossed as a contraction of *gane i tamaqu*, "my father's sister").

But of all institutional arrangements that might be adduced in explanation of the Fijian scheme, bilateral cross-cousin marriage is probably the most satisfactory. It accounts for, and that simply, the essential classifications. One perceives immediately the relevant genealogical equations: $Wi = MoBrDa = FaSiDa = BrWi$; $SiHu = MoBrSo = FaSiSo$; $Ch = MoBrDaCh = FaSiDaCh$; etc. Here, however, the matter can be approached comprehensively, from the vantage of the kin categories, which will as such bear unitary definitions in relation to cross-cousin marriage. All members of the class *wekaqu* (V) share in this connection the status of "nonmarriageable women" —that is, all sisters and female parallel cousins. All *watiqu* are "marriageable women"—that is, all are female cross-cousins. The category *taciqu* (VII) includes all those who, like myself, marry *watiqu* but not *wekaqu*—all brothers and male parallel cousins; while *tavalequ* (VIII) are all those who marry my "sisters" (*wekaqu*) but of course not my *watiqu*—that is, all male cross-cousins. The succeeding generation accordingly correlates and divides the children of intermarrying classes of my own generation: children of VII and VI are IV (*luvequ*, "children"); and children of VIII and V are II (*vugoqu*, "sister's children"). Thus the relatives my children cannot marry (IV) are opposed to my potential children-in-law (III). In the same way, terminology on my parents' generation divides parents-in-law (III, *vugoqu*) from *tinaqu* (II, "mothers") and *tamaqu* (I, "fathers")—that is, from the parents of women I cannot marry. And incidentally, we succeed in reducing category III, *vugoqu*, to a specific definition, "in-law of adjacent generation."

It is obvious that this classification works perfectly well if "sister-exchange" is additionally specified. Except for the bugaboo *vugoqu* (III), the terminology is perfectly appropriate to a dual organization of exogamous lineages. Every term save *vugoqu* specifies, as well as sex and generation status, status in one's own or the other moiety. Even as it stands, every term including *vugoqu* indicates whether the person is "own" or "in-law." Too, it is patent that the pattern as constituted is harmonious with classificatory cross-cousin marriage. I call your attention to the resemblance between the "dual organization" on ego's children's generation in this diagram and the diagram (Fig. 4.5) of classificatory cross-cousin marriage on page 61. Finally, the scheme is consistent with classificatory cross-cousin marriage only (own cross-cousin marriage not allowed), which is the rule among the Fijians who practice it. Here, however, the consistency is a logical necessity: unitary definitions of the categories cannot be given in marital terms since my own female cross-cousins are not "marriageable women"—though custom does not preclude a little playing around.

Five   *Tribal*
Economics

Although concerned with "economics," the present chapter discusses families as much as production; where it speaks of exchange it is preoccupied with kinship, and when it deals with consumption it is all about chiefs. Something more is involved than the simple point that economics is functionally related to the social and political arrangements of tribal societies. Economics is not distinguishable from these arrangements. The economy is organized by just such generalized institutions as families and lineages—"embedded" in them, as the economic historian says.[1]

An exchange of goods appears as a momentary episode in a continuous social relation. The terms of the exchange are governed by the relation of the parties to it. Different relationships, different terms. What are in the conventional wisdom of economic science "exogenous" or "noneconomic" factors, such as kinship and politics, are in the tribal reality the very organization of the economic process. Anthropological economics cannot conceive them as

---

[1] See Karl Polanyi, "Aristotle Discovers the Economy," and "The Economy as Instituted Process," in K. Polanyi, C. Arensberg, and H. Pearson, eds., *Trade and Markets in The Early Empires* (Glencoe, Ill.: The Free Press and The Falcon's Wing Press, 1957), pp. 64–94, 243–270.

external, impinging upon "the economy" from somewhere outside it. They *are* the economy, essential elements of the economic calculus and of any proper analysis of it. The matter is generally as Evans-Pritchard said of the Nuer: "One cannot treat Nuer economic relations by themselves, for they always form part of direct social relations of a general kind." [2]

The Familial Mode
of Production

Thus in tribal societies the "mode of production"—taking the phrase to include relations of production as well as material means—should be styled "domestic" or "familial," in light of the strategic position assumed by individual households. The family is to the tribal economy as the manor to the medieval European economy, or the industrial corporation to modern capitalism: each of these is the central production-institution of its time. Each, moreover, is a special way of producing, involving a characteristic division of labor and type of technology, certain property relations, definite objectives of production, and customary social and material relations with similar groups.

The domestic groups of tribal societies have not yet suffered demotion to a mere consumption status. Nor is human labor power detached from the family and, employed in an external realm, made subject to an alien organization and purpose. Production is a domestic function. The family is *as such* directly engaged in the economic process, and largely in control of it. Its own inner relations, as between husband and wife, parent and child, are relations of production. What goods the people produce, as well as how their labor is allocated, are for the most part domestic stipulations. The decisions are taken with a view to domestic needs: production is geared to familial requirements.

I hasten to add that domestic groups are not self-sufficient, although they often do produce most of what they consume. Household production is not precisely described as "production for use"; i.e., for direct consumption. Families may also produce for exchange, thus indirectly getting what they need. Still, it is "what they need" that governs output, not how much profit they can make. The interest in exchange remains a consumer interest, not a capitalist one. Perhaps the best phrase is "production for provisioning."

It would be wrong, too, to suppose that the family is necessarily a self-contained work group. Its members frequently co-operate with individuals of other households, and some tasks may be undertaken collectively at higher levels, as by lineage or village groups. "Familial mode of production" is not synonymous with "familial production." It is the regulation of production which is at issue, and its orientation or purpose. Production is principally organized by and for families, if it is not always carried on as a domestic activity.

The sovereignty of domestic groups in the domain of production rests on this: that they are constituted, equipped, entitled, and empowered to determine and fashion the societal output. Families are *constituted* for production primarily by the sexual division of labor, the sole full-time specialization

---

[2] E. E. Evans-Pritchard, *The Nuer* (Oxford: Clarendon Press, 1940), p. 90.

in the run of primitive societies. Complementary and nearly exhaustive of society's tasks, a man's work together with a woman's can provide most of the customary Good Things. Families are *equipped* to govern production by possession of the necessary tools and skills; they generally hold the everyday technical means. This control is consistent with a certain simplicity of the means, one might say a certain democracy of technology: implements that are easily made and widely available; technical skills that are common, public knowledge; uncomplicated tools that can be wielded by individuals or small groups; and productive processes that are often unitary, such that the same interested party can carry through the whole job from extraction of the natural resource to completion of the consumable product. Finally, the family is *entitled* and *empowered* to act autonomously by its access to resources of production. Not that it is the exclusive private owner of farmlands, pastures, and other natural resources. More commonly these are held by larger corporate groups, such as lineages or villages, and the family's rights are contingent on its membership in the proprietary group. The family has *usufructuary privilege*—including control of the manner of use of its share, and of disposition of the product. Rather than an impediment to family enjoyment, the investment of ownership in a larger group gives member families something of an inalienable guarantee of livelihood. No household is in the normal course excluded from direct access to the means of its own survival, any more than it is excluded from participation in the greater social structure. No expropriated class of landless paupers is characteristic of tribal societies. If expropriation occurs, it is by way of accident—as a cruel fortune of war, for instance—and not as a constituted condition of the economy.

Some tribal societies, we have seen, are ranked, but none is a class society. Standing against class formation, as it stands against economic stratification, is the system of autonomous family production. The people's hold on their own means of production is fatal to any such design of economic power. The appropriation of critical productive means by some few is precluded, and thereby the economic servility of the many others. Whatever other means tribesmen devise to elevate a man above his fellows, and they are several, this one, history's most compelling, is not open to them.

As far as the organization of production itself goes, the best word for it may be *anarchy*. The social economy is broken down into independent household existences, constituted to operate parallel to each other and in an uncoordinated way. Beyond similarities stemming from common material goals, households are not inherently brought into relation by the productive process. This allegation of primitive anarchy is not made to alarm—rest assured, it is dialectically overcome by forces of social order—but only to summarize in a forceful way the atomistic aspects of a familial mode of production. It calls attention to the lack of greater organization, of centralization in the setup of production. It testifies to a minimal organic interdependence, to limited cooperation through specialization. It speaks too of diffuse, local, familial control of production, and of self-centered domestic decisions.

In one respect the primitive anarchy surpasses the disarray of competitive small-scale private enterprise. Compared with the tribal condition, capitalist free enterprise is the apotheosis of order. Organizing a vast division of labor, the competitive market economy embodies at least continuous action and reaction, systematic adjustments in production set off by variations in price. Nor is "glut" occasioned by a headlong rush of independent entrepreneurs toward profitable lines the recurrent weakness of primitive anarchy. If anything, the tribal crisis is underproduction—not enough goods forthcoming from the several domestic establishments, not enough for their own good, or for the good of society.

While it seems a feasible arrangement to vest control of their own provisioning in household groups, it does not always succeed. For these groups may be unable to muster the manpower. The small domestic labor force—in the first place, perhaps unfavorably constituted, with too many unproductive dependents relative to productive workers—is often sorely beset. Its working adults are vulnerable to incapacitating injury, disease, and an early death, and the women to an occasional pregnancy. These handicaps, or even slight disadvantages in luck or skill, translate themselves into serious food shortages. If left to "go it alone," the household economy proves inadequate: some families at any given time, and any given family at some times, can probably look forward to the prospect of an empty granary.

Contributing to this dismal outlook is another factor, the importance of which cannot be exaggerated: the economy is not organized for sustained production even in normal times. A domestic mode of production is a mode of *domestic* production. Directed toward supplying the family with its customary stock of consumables, it has built-in limits on output, and no inherent propensity to evoke continuous work or surpassing wealth. In more familiar terms, incentive to produce a surplus is lacking. On the contrary, the domestic mode of production would inhibit surplus production. When no household need is in sight, or none that could not be met by some future effort, the normal tendency is to leave off working. Production ceases when the domestic quota is filled for the time being. The economic organization implies this definite ceiling on output—beyond that it is "a fetter on the means of production."

Here the classic distinction between "production for use" (i.e., provisioning) and "production for exchange" (i.e., profit) becomes meaningful. The competitive market is an eternal dynamo, perhaps not always in working order, but at least designed to generate intensive currents of output. On the producer's side, the incentive to profitable enlargement is continuous, as a matter of jungle survival. But perhaps most of us are more familiar with the push (and pull) on the consumer. The market makes available a dazzling array of products, good things in unlimited quantity and variety, each with its clarion price-tag call: "this is all it takes to have me." A man's reach is then inevitably beyond his grasp, for one never has enough to buy everything. Before the judgment of the market, the consumer stands condemned to *scarcity*, and so to a life sentence at hard labor. Nor is there any reprieve in acquiring things. To participate in a market economy is an inevitable tragedy: what began in inadequacy will end in deprivation. For every acquisition is simultaneously a deprivation—of something else that could have been had instead. To buy one thing is to deny yourself another. Should one choose to spend his scarce resources on the latest Ford, he cannot also have the newest Plymouth (and I judge from the TV commercials that the deprivations involved are more than just material).

The competitive market combines scarcity, demand, work, and supply in a riotous turmoil of creation. Now let thoughts rest on this serene contrast, derived from observation of the Indonesian village economy, a peasant system to be sure but in the particulars at issue not different from a tribal economy.

> Another respect in which an Eastern differs from a Western society is the fact that *needs are very limited*. This is connected with the limited development of exchange, with the fact that most people have to provide for themselves, that families have to be content with what they are able to produce themselves, so that needs necessarily have to remain modest in quantity and quality. Another consequence of this is that the economic motive does not work continuously. Therefore . . . economic activity is also intermittent. Western economy tends in a diametrically opposite direction, its starting point being the idea of limitless needs in comparison with which means are always limited, so that the economic subject must always, when, satisfying his wants, make a choice and impose limits on himself.[3]

The constraints of the household economy are, however, overcome in tribal societies—or else the society is overcome. It is, after all, a matter of survival. Families that do not support themselves are either supplied by others or go under. The need for a public economy may be just as serious; that is, some means of subsidizing and organizing such collective enterprises as irrigation construction and such activities as religious ceremony and warfare. A society can expire for lack of these too, and the domestic stranglehold on production bids fair to arrange just such an end—were it not for counteracting institutions such as kinship, or chieftainship.

The kinship nexus relegates economic anarchy to a contradiction lurking in the background. Caught up with others in a community of kinship, a family is hard-pressed to maintain the luxury of domestic self-interest, especially when relatives next door haven't enough to eat. If the familial mode of production generates centripetal economic forces, kinship sets off centrifugal ones, propelling goods out of the household for remedial distribution to the destitute. Urgent goods flow along kinship lines from the haves to the have-nots. Nor does the "feedback" necessarily come in the form of grateful reciprocation, but perhaps in additional production by the donor, now saddled with the upkeep of others as well as his own house. In other words, kinship responsibilities may force effective producers to extend their output above and beyond the call of domestic duty. More than an incentive to charity, kinship gives the spur to productivity.

The organization of authority likewise stands against the organization of production. Power invades the humble home, subverting familial economic autonomy and contending successfully against domestic underproduction. The public economic role of tribal authorities demands that they thus impose upon the underlying population. Big-men and chiefs are compelled to relieve shortages among the people—just like ordinary kinsmen but even more so, for the tribal leader is a paragon among kinsmen and his concern for community welfare is a kind of centralization of kinship morality. Besides bread, there are certain circuses. Here local authorities play the impresario, putting

---

[3] J. H. Boeke, *Economics and Economic Policy of Dual Societies* (New York: Institute of Pacific Relations, 1953), p. 39.

on main community events: the spectacular rituals, public works, ceremonious exchanges with other groups. "I think that throughout the world," Malinowski wrote, "we would find that the relations between economics and politics are of the same type. The chief, everywhere, acts as a tribal banker, collecting food, storing it, and protecting it, and then using it for the benefit of the whole community." [4]

To function in this capacity, a chief must apply pressure on the household economies within his sphere, forcing them to raise their production sights or summoning labor from them "for the benefit of the whole community." Leadership is one of the great productive forces. It acts to intensify familial production, to congeal by political pressure a material surplus, and, in disposing of this fund, to float the community as a going concern. Different systems of tribal authority, as we shall see, develop varying impacts on the domestic economy, thus different coefficients of production and surplus accumulation. Quite apart from technological improvements, political transformation can play the decisive role in economic development.

A word on "the condition of the working class." Working conditions are hardly ideal, and perhaps tribesmen ought to have a union, but about the hours they needn't complain. It is said that an American is hardly ever beyond hearing the hum of some motor or another. The rhythmic purr of machinery in any event has become for us the Great Metronome of Life, to which all human tempos are adjusted. Regular, repetitive work, the "daily grind," is the American plan. Here again tribal peoples differ from us notably. Their labor is more episodic and diversified. It is in total less than ours. It is also not so inhuman.

In a household economy, as Boeke says, the economic motive does not work continuously; therefore, neither do people. There are after all two roads to satisfaction, to reducing the gap between means and ends: producing much or desiring little. Oriented toward providing a modest supply of consumables, the household economy takes the latter, Zen course. Their needs, we say, are limited. Economic activity therefore does not break into a galloping compulsion, goaded by an interminable sense of inadequacy (i.e., a "scarcity of means"). Work is instead intermittent, sporadic, discontinuous, ceasing for the moment when not required for the moment. To this ordinary irregularity a neolithic economy adds long periods of "seasonal unemployment" following the harvest, or at least a depressed level of activity implying a "concealed unemployment." Take the eight-hour day, five-day week, forty-eight week year as the American standard. Then tribal peoples work less than we do, as well as less regularly. They probably also sleep more in the daytime. Certain orthodox views of evolution are better turned around: the amount of work per capita *increases* in proportion to technological advance, and the amount of leisure *decreases*.

Nor is tribal labor alienated labor. We have seen it is not alienated from the means of production or from the product. Indeed, the tribesman's relation to productive means and finished products often exceeds ownership as we understand it, moving beyond mundane possession to a mystic attachment.

[4] Bronislaw Malinowski, "Anthropology as the Basis of Social Sciences," in Cattel, Cohen and Travers, eds., *Human Affairs* (London. Macmillan, 1937), p. 232.

The land is a spiritual value, a beneficent Source—the home of the ancestors, "the plain of one's bones," Hawaiians say. And the things a man makes and habitually uses are expressions of himself, perhaps so imbued with his genius that their ultimate disposition can be only his own grave.

These mystical associations reflect another aspect of labor: that it is not alienated from man himself, detachable from his social being and transactable as so many units of depersonalized labor-power. A man works, produces, in his capacity as a social person, as a husband and father, brother and lineage mate, member of a clan, a village. Labor is not implemented apart from these existences, as if it were a different existence. "Worker" is not a status in itself, nor "labor" a true category of tribal economics. Said differently, work is organized by relations "noneconomic" in the conventional sense, belonging rather to the general organization of society. Work is an expression of pre-existing kin and community relations, the exercise of these relations. This remains true of arrangements that seem otherwise like hire, where a man engages to work for another. "The situation is phrased [by the Abelam of New Guinea] in terms of kinship obligation, 'she is my sister, therefore I prepare the sago with her,' and *not* in some such phrase as 'she will give me sago, therefore I help her.' " [5]

But then, a man is what he does, and what he does is what he is. Incapable of selling himself as independent of himself, a man is not by work detached from his existence as a dutiful kinsman, citizen of the community, and an intelligent being capable of art and joy. Work is not divorced from life. There is no "job," no time and place where one spends most of one's time not being oneself. Nor are work and life related as means to end (as they often are for us): the former a necessary evil tolerated for the sake of the latter, "living," which is something to do after business hours, on your *own* time, if you have the energy. The Industrial Revolution split work from life. The reintegration has not yet been achieved. In the interim, the loss of primitive human integration is a justifiable lament of romantic criticism, and the alienation of labor a penetrating cry of revolutionary pain:

What, then, constitutes the alienation of labour? First, the fact that labour is *external* to the worker, i.e., it does not belong to his essential being; that in his work, therefore, he does not affirm himself but denies himself, does not feel content but unhappy, does not develop freely his physical and mental energy but mortifies his body and ruins his mind. The worker therefore only feels himself outside his work, and in his work he feels outside himself. He is at home when he is not working, and when he is working he is not at home. His labour is therefore not voluntary, but coerced; it is *forced labour*. It is therefore not the satisfaction of a need; it is merely a *means* to satisfy needs external to it. Its alien character emerges clearly in the fact that as soon as no physical or other compulsion exists, labour is shunned like the plague. . . . Lastly, the external character of labour for the worker appears in the fact that it is not his own, but someone else's, that it does not belong to him, that in it he belongs . . . to another. Just as in religion the spontaneous activity of the human imagination, of the human brain and the human heart, operates

[5] Phyllis M. Kaberry, "The Abelam Tribe, Sepik District, New Guinea: A Preliminary Report," *Oceania*, XI (1940–41), 351.

independently of the individual—that is, operates on him as an alien, divine or diabolical activity—in the same way the worker's activity is not his spontaneous activity. It belongs to another; it is the loss of his self.[6]

But in the tribal condition, labor is not alienated from man or from the things on which he works. It is rather a bridge between the two. The consummation of labor's inalienability is a mystic union between man and the objects of his labor. Land symbolically represents the producers, and the products of their efforts animistically embody them. Labor is the procurer of a symbolic intercourse with things. And, Marx's religious metaphor notwithstanding, perhaps it was just thus that religion was conceived.

Exchange and Kinship

Exchange in tribal societies is, like work, governed by "direct social relations of a general kind." It is instigated often as an expression of such relations, and constrained always by the kinship and community standing of the parties concerned. The greater part of tribal exchange, therefore, is like the lesser part of our own—in a class with the gift-giving and hospitality we practice with social intimates. Contaminated as they are by social considerations, these reciprocal gestures are conceived by us as "noneconomic," qualitatively different from the main run of proper exchange and confined to a sphere where whoever saw fit to do business on the principle of devil-take-the-hindmost would be cordially directed to go to the devil himself. But in the tribes, just as "labor" does not exist as a differentiated activity independent of the worker's other social capacities, so exchange does not exist apart from "noneconomic" relations. Better said, there is an economic aspect to every social relationship. Father-son, maternal uncle-nephew, chief-follower: each implies a mode of exchange of one kind or another, consistent in its material terms with its social terms. Thus, from a relative "you can get it wholesale," and, from a close relative, perhaps for free.

On a more abstract level: the tribal exchange scheme is constructed from the scheme of social segmentation. Each group in the segmentary hierarchy is in the perspective of its participants a sector of social relationships, more or less solidary and sociable—more in the inner spheres of home and community, progressively less as one proceeds toward the intertribal outer darkness. As I suggested in an earlier passage (p. 19), each sector implies appropriate norms of reciprocity. Differences thus appear in the way people deal with each other, according to the way they are socially divided from each other. The tribal scheme of segmentation sets up a sectoral scheme of reciprocities.

But is this not poorly stated? Normally the term "reciprocity" does not admit of degrees. Yet ethnography will support us here. Reciprocity is not always a one-for-one exchange. There is, in fact, a complex continuum of variations in the directness and equivalence of exchange. The subtleties of reciprocal exchange appear especially when one concentrates singularly on the material transaction, leaving aside "reciprocity" in the sense of a broad social

---

[6] Karl Marx, *Economic and Philosophic Manuscripts of 1844* (Moscow: Foreign Languages Publishing House, 1961), pp. 72–73.

principle or moral norm of give-and-take. Observable at one end of the spectrum is assistance freely given, the small currency of everyday kinship, friendship, and neighborly relations, the "pure gift" Malinowski called it, regarding which an explicit demand for reciprocation would be as unthinkable as it is unsociable—although it would be equally bad form not to bestow similar casual favors in return, if and when it is possible. Toward the middle of the continuum stand balanced exchanges, in which a fair and immediate trade is right behavior, as for example when kinsmen come from a distance seeking food and bearing gifts. And at the far end of the spectrum: self-interested seizure, appropriation by chicane or force requited only by an equal and opposite reaction on the principle of *lex talionis*—"negative reciprocity," Alvin Gouldner calls it.[7]

Consider that the extremes are notably positive and negative in a moral sense, and the intervals between them not only so many gradations of material balance but of sociability. The distance between the poles of reciprocity is social distance. "Unto a stranger," says the Old Testament, "thou mayest lend upon usury; but unto thy brother thou shalt not lend upon usury." The same applies in the wilds of New Guinea: "A trader always cheats people. For this reason intra-regional trade is rather frowned upon while intertribal trade gives to the [Kapauku] businessman prestige as well as profit."[8] Thorstein Veblen framed the common underlying principle. "Gain at the cost of other communities," he wrote, "particularly communities at a distance, and more especially such as are felt to be aliens, is not obnoxious to the standards of homebred use and wont."

In his book *The Hunters*, Professor Service defined the end points on the continuum of reciprocity—"generalized" and "negative" reciprocity—and also the mid-point—"balanced" reciprocity.[9] In the interest of describing the sectoral economy of tribal societies, we briefly recapitulate this typology:

> 1. *Generalized reciprocity.* These transactions are at least putatively altruistic, on the lines of assistance given and, if possible and necessary, assistance returned. Aside from the "pure gifts" mentioned before, other concrete forms of generalized reciprocity appear in ethnographic accounts as "sharing," "hospitality," "token gifts," "mutual aid," and "generosity." Obligatory gifts to kinsmen and chiefs ("kinship dues" and "chiefly dues") as well as *noblesse oblige* are less sociable but, without stretching the point too much, in the same class.
>
> At the extreme, say voluntary food-sharing among very close relatives—or for its logical value one might think of a mother suckling her child—the expectation of a direct material return is unseemly, at the most implicit. The social side of the relation overwhelms the material and in a way conceals it, as if it were of no account. Reckoning is simply not proper. Not that there is no obligation to reciprocate, but the expectation of reciprocity is left indefinite, unspecified as to time, quantity, and quality. As it works in practice, the time of reciprocation and the value of return gifts

---

[7] Alvin W. Gouldner, "The Norm of Reciprocity: A Preliminary Statement," *American Sociological Review*, XXV (1960), 161–178.

[8] Leopold Pospisil, *Kapauka Papuans and Their Law*, Yale University Publications in Anthropology, No. 54 (New Haven: Yale University Press, 1958), 127.

[9] Elman Service, *The Hunters* (Englewood Cliffs, N.J.: Prentice-Hall, 1966).

are not only conditional on what the donor gave, but also on what he needs and when, and likewise what the recipient can afford to give him and when. The obligation to reciprocate is diffuse: when necessary to the donor and/or possible for the recipient. The requital thus may be very soon, or then again, never. There are people—the widowed, the old, the impaired—who in the fullness of time remain incapable of helping themselves or others. Yet the obligations to them of close kin may not falter. A sustained one-way flow is a good pragmatic sign of generalized reciprocity. Failure to reciprocate, or to give just as much as was received, does not cause the original giver of things to stop: the goods move one way, in favor of the have-not, for a long time.

2. *Balanced reciprocity*. Direct exchange: the return is made straight off and is equivalent in value to the goods received. The perfect type of balanced reciprocity, a simultaneous exchange of identical things, is not only conceivable but ethnographically documented in certain marital transactions between bride's and groom's kinsmen, blood-brotherhood pacts, and peace agreements. More loosely, "balanced reciprocity" may be applied where goods of commensurate worth or utility should be given in return within a customary finite period or short run. Many of the "gift-exchanges" of which ethnographers write, as well as much of the "trade," "barter," and "buying" with "primitive money" belong in this class of reciprocity.

Balanced reciprocity is less "personal" than generalized reciprocity, so from our distorted vantage, "more economic." The people deal as parties of separate economic and social interests. The material aspect of the bargain is as important as the social, and there has to be some reckoning, more or less precise, because accounts have to be balanced. So the pragmatic test here is an inability to tolerate one-way flows: the relations between people are disrupted when one reneges, fails to make a *quid pro quo* within a limited time period—like the feeling a hostess gets when a fairly distant acquaintance she has invited once or twice to dinner doesn't "in all this time" invite her. Among close friends there would not be the same calculation.

3. *Negative reciprocity*. This is the attempt to get something for nothing: transactions opened and conducted toward net utilitarian advantage. In other words, what we might consider sound business principles. It appears on the ethnographic record occasionally as "bargaining" or "haggling," or even in more unsociable forms as "gambling," "chicanery," "theft," and other varieties of seizure. The participants in all instances confront each other not merely as distinct but opposed interests, each looking to maximize his position at the other's expense. Bargaining with an eye to the main chance is one of the more sociable forms. From this, negative reciprocity ranges through various degrees of cunning, guile, stealth, and violence to the finesse of a well-conducted horse raid. Like generalized reciprocity, the "reciprocation" is conditional again, but in an opposite way: contingent on mustering enough countervailing pressure or guile to serve or, better, enhance one's own interests.

It is a long way from a suckling child to a Plains Indian horse-raid. But the exchanges of even a single tribal society can grade into each other along the whole span. Not, however, in a random way. After all, one suckles one's own child and steals horses from some other outfit. The disposition to practice one or another mode of reciprocity is sectorally organized. It is close kin who are inclined to share, to enter into generalized reciprocity, and distant and non-kin who trade and horse-trade. The need to strike a balance becomes compulsory in proportion to kinship distance, lest relations break off altogether, for with distance and separation of-interests there can be little tolerance for gain and loss, even as there is little inclination to extend oneself on another's behalf. As far as non-kinsmen are concerned—those "other people" who are perhaps not even "people"—no quarter need be given and none is asked; but let the buyer beware.

The play of sectoral distinctions on reciprocity is complicated by the influence of spatial distance on measures of "kinship distance" (see p. 18). Close kinsmen usually live nearby and distant kinsmen far away, because kinsmen who live nearby are reckoned close in a sociological sense whereas those who live at a distance are distant kinsmen. The rule is subject to several exceptions; *e.g.*, fellow-clansmen or genealogically close relatives who happen to reside in other places. These may be treated economically as if in a nearer social sphere. Otherwise, reciprocity marches in character with segmentary distance.

Probably all this has been easy to understand—because in fact it is perfectly applicable to our own society. It is only more significant in tribal society. Partly because kinship is more significant there. Even the category "non-kinsman" is defined by kinship, that is, as the logical boundary of the class. Among ourselves, non-kinsman is usually also a positive status relation of some kind: doctor-patient, policeman-citizen, classmates, professional colleagues, etc. But for them non-kinsman is ordinarily the negation of community or tribal-ism—thus often synonymous with "stranger" and "enemy." The economic relation is accordingly a simple negation of kinship reciprocities; other institutional norms need not be invoked.

For a general appreciation, then, of the play of reciprocity among tribesmen, we superimpose the society's sectoral plan on the reciprocity continuum (Fig. 5.1). The relations of each social sphere are more solidary than relations of the next, more peripheral sector. Reciprocity thus tends toward balance and chicane in proportion to sectoral distance. In each sector, certain modes of exchange are dominant or characteristic. Generalized reciprocity prevails in the narrower spheres and plays out in the wider; balanced reciprocity is characteristic of intermediate segmentary relations; negative reciprocity is the mode of peripheral, especially inter-tribal, exchange.

This profile of exchange is purely hypothetical. Incorporated within the particular segmentary structures of particular societies, the spectrum of reciprocities is variously modified. To adjust our standardized conception to the variations posed by real societies, it will be necessary to move the balanced reciprocity "mid-point" inward in some cases, outward in others, reflecting narrower or wider fields of generalized exchange. Indeed, just such pulsations of generosity may materialize within the same tribe over a period of time and changing circumstance. Beset by declining food supplies, it is common for tribesmen (and not only tribesmen) to meet the threat by a double-barreled intensification of community solidarity and economic cooperation. People help each other out as they can and, during the shortage, generalized reciprocity is

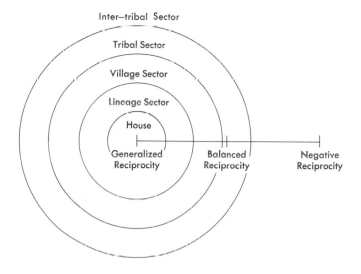

Figure 5.1. Reciprocity and
kinship-residential sectors.

Inter—tribal Sector

Tribal Sector

Village Sector

Lineage Sector

House

Generalized   Balanced   Negative
Reciprocity   Reciprocity   Reciprocity

stretched beyond its normal social sphere. Yet, if the shortage proves prolonged and severe, the structure of solidarities may prove unable to bear the
strain: in the final crisis households reassert their self-interest, and people who
had shared food through the first stages of disaster display now indifference to
each others' plight, if they do not hasten a mutual downfall by guile, haggle,
and theft.

Even as a normal rule, different societies draw the line on helpful sharing at
different points. Some peoples, we are tempted to say, are selfish, willing perhaps to render assistance to a few intimates while reluctant to make even a
quid pro quo with anyone else, including kinsmen of nearby places. Said in
sociology, the segmentary system develops marked cleavages at lower levels,
such that small local groups of kinsmen, highly solidary within, maintain a
posture of sustained hostility toward all others. The people's selfishness, which
is to say, the limited compass of generalized reciprocity, reflects then their
splintered social condition. On the other hand, inter-tribal symbiosis involving
regular exchange of important specialized products may inhibit the propensity
to "gain at the cost of communities at a distance—especially such as are felt
to be aliens," and instead extend fair dealing (balanced reciprocity) into
peripheral zones.

This becoming honesty toward foreigners is promoted in the interest of
peace and continued trade, which are otherwise quite vulnerable to disruption
by hostile haggling. The check on sharp practice is imposed by special institutions of border exchange, by means that sometimes look so preposterous as to
seem some kind of game the natives play, but whose design manifestly im-
munizes an important economic interdependence against a fundamental social
divergence. Silent trade, as between Bantu agriculturalists and Pygmy hunters
in the Congo, is a case in point: good relations are maintained by preventing
direct relations. The external "trade-partnership," of which Melanesia affords
classic examples, is even more prevalent than silent trade. A continuing compact between individuals of different communities or tribes, perhaps established along lines of classificatory kinship, the trade-partnership not only
constitutes a binding exchange agreement but encapsulates it in solidary social
relations. Internal relations are, as it were, projected across tribal boundaries.
Chicanery is thus outlawed and customary standards of equivalence come into

force. Reciprocity may then lean over backwards, the balanced exchange tempered by elements of generosity. The trade is phrased is gift-giving between kinsmen. Delays in reciprocation are tolerated—or even enjoined, that the transaction not look like mere trading—and hospitality in food and lodging accompanies the formal exchange of trade goods. Inter-tribal symbiosis, in short, alters the propositions of our hypothetical model. Put in the context of a narrower co-membership sphere, the exchange is rendered both peaceful and equitable.

It seems useful in concluding this discussion of sectoral variations in reciprocity to adduce a concrete example to show how these variations may be discerned in anthropological accounts. The villagers of Busama, on the Huon Gulf of New Guinea, enjoy an extensive trade with other coastal communities of the Gulf and also with inlanders of the region. But a difference appears in the way Busama deal with these two categories of outsiders, for the maritime trade-partners of the Busama are kinsmen, whereas the inlanders, with whom trade is comparatively recent, are not. This then is one sectoral break in the mode of exchange; another is set at the boundaries of Busama village itself, where the people practice a generosity uncommon in any external sphere.

> H. Ian Hogbin, the ethnographer, first notes the contrast between the more personal exchange with coastal partners and the more commercial transactions with inlanders, writing of the latter: "The parties seem slightly ashamed . . . and conclude their arrangements outside the village. *Commerce, it is considered, should be carried on away from where people live.* . . . The Busama sum up the situation by saying that the maritime people give one another presents but insist on a proper return from the bushmen. The basis of the distinction is that on the coast activities are confined to relatives, but so few of the beach folk have kinsmen in the hill country that most transactions take place . . . between comparative strangers. [But] . . . every coastal native [including Busama] has kinsmen in some of the other shore villages. . . . When trading by sea it is with these, and these only, that he makes exchanges. *Kinship ties and bargaining are considered to be incompatible,* and all goods are handed over as free gifts offered from motives of sentiment. . . . Most of the visitors go home with items at least as valuable as those with which they came. *Indeed, the closer the kinship bond the greater the host's generosity is.* . . . A careful count is kept, however, and the score is afterwards made even." Note now the distinction between this trade and rates of exchange within the village: It is significant that when a Busama acquired a string bag from a fellow villager, as has recently become possible, he always gives twice what he would pay to a more distant relative [i.e., trade-kinsman] on the north coast. "One is ashamed," the people explain, "to treat those with whom one is familiar like tradesmen." [10]

Political Economy

Differences of rank, as much as distances of kinship, suppose an economic relation and an appropriate mode of exchange. Not the least among nobility's privileges is the economic one, the lord's due; nor is *noblesse oblige*

[10] H. Ian Hogbin, *Transformation Scene* (London: Routledge & Kegan Paul, 1951), pp. 83–86 (my emphases).

the least of obligations. Thus the dues and duties fall on both sides of a relation of rank: both high and low have their claims on each other. And indeed feudal terminology does not do justice to the economic equity of kinship ranking. In its own historic setting *noblesse oblige* hardly canceled the *droits du seigneur*; in tribal society social inequality is more the organization of economic equality, and high position often only secured or maintained by o'ercrowing generosity. Perhaps the best way I can describe the economic ethics of a primitive nobility is to repeat the response of a chief of the Tongan Islands upon his hearing a white man extol the virtues of money:

> Finow replied that the explanation did not satisfy him; he still thought it a foolish thing that people should place a value on money, when they either could not or would not apply it to any useful [physical] purpose. "If," said he, "it were made of iron, and could be converted into knives, axes and chisels, there would be some sense in placing a value on it; but as it is, I see none. . . . Certainly, money is much handier, and more convenient, but then, as it will not spoil by being kept, people will store it up, instead of sharing it out, as a chief ought to do, and thus become selfish; whereas, if provisions were the principal property of man, and it ought to be, as being both the most useful and the most necessary, he could not store it up, for it would spoil, and so he would be obliged either to exchange it away for something else useful, or share it to his neighbors, and inferior chiefs and dependents, for nothing. I understand now [he concluded] what it is that makes the Papalangis [the Europeans] so selfish —it is this money." [11]

The tribal leader's claims on his followers and theirs on him are interdependent. A chief's demand for goods and services in turn obligates him, opens him to requests from those who answer his. Conversely, the chief's assistance to his people is his lien on them. In a word, the economic relation between mighty and lowly is reciprocal. And it is in the genre of generalized reciprocity, phrased as assistance with the return left indefinite, but tempered often by power, for goods are in truth *yielded* to people in authority and their favors may have to be humbly *solicited*. It seems good sociology if bad punning to say the mode of exchange is "akin" to generalized reciprocity, with the chief acting in a capacity of superior kinsman—the "father of his people." On the other hand, a moderate exposure to Westerners may put the people in mind of another institution, the self-same as occurred to Malinowski when he described the chief as "a tribal banker": thus, the Solomon islander explained to the missionary that the chief's store of wealth is "the 'panga,' the 'bank' of the village because it is drawn on for communal purposes such as feasts or the payments of blood money." [12]

The "economic basis" of tribal politics is chiefly generosity, at one stroke an act of positive morality and a laying of indebtedness upon the underlying population. Or, to take a more complete view, the political order is underwritten by a centralized circulation of goods, flowing toward the top of the social pyramid and down again, with each presentation not only implying a

[11] William Mariner, *An Account of the Tongan Islands in the South Pacific Ocean*, 3rd ed., John Martin, ed. (Edinburgh: Constable, 1827), Vol. 1, 213–214.

[12] W. G. Ivens, *Melanesians of the Southeast Solomon Islands* (London: Kegan, Paul, Trench, Trubner, 1927), p. 32.

relation of rank but, as a generalized gift not directly requited, compelling a loyalty.

One discerns two different ways of thus putting reciprocity at the service of hierarchy. In certain tribes the system of rank already exists, the chiefs installed in office and the people in submission, a place for everybody and everybody in their place. Here reciprocity between chiefs and people follows from established rights and privileges, and once set going the exchange has redundant effects on the rank system. But in a great many tribal societies, dominance is a personal capacity rather than a constituted position, and generalized reciprocity is enlisted in its achievement. In the first case, the existing rank order evokes certain economic relations; in the second, certain economic relations are used to evoke an order of rank. The first is the way of true chieftainship, operating on the principle, "to be noble is to be generous." The second is the way of the big-man, working from the corollary proposition that "to be generous is to be noble."

If it is true that a particular social relation suggests a consistent mode of exchange, it is also true ("by the same token") that a kind of exchange generates a consistent social relation. If friends make gifts, gifts make friends. Or, more appropriate to the present context, "gifts make slaves," as the Eskimo say, "just as whips make dogs." The big-men of Melanesian communities and so-called "chiefs" among Plains Indians, insofar as economic dealings are involved in their prominence, utilize just this connection between gifts and rank to launch their careers. They turn economic imbalance into political inequality. An unrequited gift, as Bushmen would say, "creates a something between people." At least it engenders a continuity in their relation, during all that period it is not reciprocated. More than that, the recipient of a favor is in an equivocal social position—in debt. The "norm of reciprocity," Alvin Gouldner observes, "makes two interrelated minimal demands: (1) people should help those who have helped them, and (2) people should not injure those who have helped them." [13] These demands are as compelling in the clan-territories of the New Guinea Highlands as in the streets of Middletown: "Gifts [among the Gahuku of New Guinea] have to be repaid. They constitute a debt, and until discharged the relationship of the individuals involved is in a state of imbalance. The debtor has to act circumspectly toward those who have this advantage over him or otherwise risk ridicule." [14] Thus, generosity creates leadership by creating followership.

Calculated generosity is the making of a Melanesian big-man. In the end it is also his undoing, and a limitation on the whole political and economic system in which he is the central figure. Other skills and personal qualities are often required for prestige: magical power, oratorical ability, perhaps bravery; but the economic maneuvers are usually decisive: amassing goods—pigs, vegetable foods, and shell monies—and distributing them in ways that build a name for cavalier generosity. By informal private assistance to people of his locale, a rising big-man develops about him a coterie of lesser men. Obligated to him, these people are responsive to his harangues, and, what is most critical, their production is put at his disposition. Culling goods from his faction, the

[13] Gouldner, *op. cit.*, p. 171.

[14] K. E. Read, "Leadership and Consensus in a New Guinea Society," *American Anthropologist*, LXI (1959), 429.

big-man sponsors great public feasts and giveaways notably involving people from other places and their big-men. He becomes thus a "man of renown," a man of influence if not exactly authority over a greater or lesser extent of the tribe.[15]

Getting a faction together is the key. Any ambitious man who can gather a following can inaugurate a societal career. The up-and-coming Melanesian big-man depends initially on a small core of followers, mainly his own household and nearest relatives. Upon these people he can prevail economically: he capitalizes in the beginning on kinship dues and by finessing the relations of generalized reciprocity appropriate among close kinsmen. At an early phase, a big-man will seek to enlarge his own household, especially by getting more wives. The more wives he has, the more pigs. (The connection between wives and pigs is functional, not identical: with more women gardening there will be more pig-feed and more swine-herds.) Each new marriage also creates another set of affinal relatives from whom he can exact support. But a leader's career goes into "take-off" when he is able to bring other men and their households into his faction, harnessing their production to his ambition. Usually this is done by helping them in some big way, as to put them forever in his debt. Paying bridewealth on behalf of a young man is a common technique.

Malinowski had a felicitous phrase for what the big-man is doing: amassing a "fund of power." A big-man is one who uses and creates social relations that give him leverage on others' production and the ability to siphon off an excess product. He transcends the fragmented household economy and, impelled by his own ambition, promotes society's interests. For in the public distribution of his funds of power, the big-man initiates a combination of groups and an organization of functions quite beyond ordinary ken. The context of the giveaway may be a religious ceremony, the construction of a local clubhouse, a ritual exchange between groups or a dance. These testaments to a big-man's status happen to bring together people from all around: the big-man fashions supralocal organization. In tribes normally segmented into small independent groups, he at least temporarily widens the sphere of economics, politics, and ceremony.

Yet always this greater societal organization depends on the lesser factional organization, and especially it depends on the ceilings on economic mobilization set by relations between big-men and their subordinates.

The personal bond between leader and follower is a serious weakness of this political economy. A personal loyalty has to be carefully constructed and periodically reinforced. If there is discontent it is more easily severed than, say, the more structured subordination of lineage member to lineage chief. Shifting dispositions and magnetisms of ambitious men in a region induce fluctuations in factions, perhaps even some overlapping of them. The death of a big-man can precipitate a regional political crisis: his faction dissolves in whole or in part and the people regroup, it may be along new lines, around aspiring

---

[15] The big-man's command ability, however, is limited to his own faction. Beyond that his influence is exerted through relations with other local big-men. He does not order the latter's people about, lest he meet the response, "Do it yourself. I'm not *your* fool. . . ." See Douglas Oliver, A *Solomon Islands Society* (Cambridge: Harvard University Press, 1955), p. 408.

big-men. The polity is unstable: in its superstructure a flux of rising and falling leaders, in its substructure of enlarging and contracting factions. Most important, however, the possibility of their desertion inhibits a leader's ability to forceably push up his followers' output. Indeed as it generates momentum, a big-man's quest for the summits of renown is likely to bring out a contradiction in his relation to followers. He finds himself encouraging defection, or even an egalitarian rebellion, by encouraging production.

One side of the Melanesian contradiction is the initial reciprocity between a big-man and his people. They give their help in return for his, and for the goods they contribute to public circulation through him, other goods (from other factions) flow back to them by the same channel. But, on the other side, a cumulative enlargement of renown forces the big-man to substitute extortion for reciprocity. Jealous of his increasing reputation, a big-man comes under increasing pressure to extract goods from his followers, to delay reciprocities owing them, and to deflect incoming goods back into external circulation. Success in a competition of renown with other big-men particularly undermines internal-factional reciprocities, for the final measure of success is to give one's rivals more pigs and food than they can hope to reciprocate. But then, the faction of the triumphant big-man is compelled to "eat the leader's renown" in return for their productive efforts. At this juncture, let the leader beware. The bigger he gets, the more politic for him to ease the pressure on his faction, which is to say, to curb his drive for funds of power. The alternative is to invite dissatisfaction, defection or, as a last resort, destruction at the hands of his own people. When one Mote, a big-man of the Kapauku tribe (West Irian), was despatched by certain close relatives because he "was not generous enough," he left this world with the cry of "death to tyrants" ringing in his ears: "You should not be the only rich man, we should all be the same, therefore you only stay equal with us." [16]

But whether by his own death or his own restraint, a damper is put eventually on a big-man's career. Evoking internal contradictions, the Melanesian big-man system thus defeats its own development. It sets a limit on the intensification of political authority, on the intensification of household production by socio-political means, and on the diversion of domestic output to the support of wider organization.

Further eastward in the Pacific, the great Polynesian chiefdoms of Hawaii, Tahiti and Tonga, although operating on a comparable technical base, managed to move beyond these limits. The Polynesian societies discovered their own contradictions, found their own plateau, but not before the political economy was carried to a higher level—under the aegis of powerful chiefs.

These chiefs did not make their positions in society; they were installed in societal positions. Theirs was the power of office. Indeed some of the very qualities of leadership that had to reside in men in Melanesia, that had to be personally demonstrated, were in Polynesia socially ascribed to rank and office. The magic a Melanesian big-man might be called upon to display, a Polynesian ruling chief inherited by divine descent as the *mana* sanctifying his rule and protecting his person against the hands of the commonalty. A New Guinea big-man had to master the compelling oratorical style; a Tongan chief had a

---

[16] Pospisil, *op. cit.*, p. 80.

trained "talking chief" whose voice was the chief's command. Most significant in this regard were the economic powers of the Polynesian ruling chief. Master of his people and "owner" (in a titular sense) of the land and sea, the chief's call on his people's labor and goods was only the chief's due. Political mobilization of the household economy did not depend on *de novo* creation by the leader of personal obligations. The presentation of first fruits of major harvests to priests and chiefs was a customary obligation laid on each gardener—on pain of supernatural punishment, or, perchance, selection as this year's sacrificial victim. By interdiction (*tabu*) on lands or seas of his domain, a ruling chief reserved their yield for collective purposes. And consider this implication of the tabu: it raises domestic production, for in the absence of a prohibition on standing crops further labor would not have been necessary. Chieftainship generates domestic surpluses, and a chiefly levy upon the domestic economy underwrites the public polity. This, moreover, on a scale beyond the conception of a tribal big-man, involving thousands of people, whose compliance was not personally dunned but structurally exacted.

The accumulation of funds of power and their redistribution was the underpinning of Polynesian politics. I use Polynesian examples here because the descriptions are good and I am familiar with them, but in respect of their redistributive activities Polynesian chiefs are at most exemplary and not at all unique. With a few minor modifications, the following eighteenth-century account of the Creek Indians (Southeast United States) could be interpolated in a book on the Maori of New Zealand:

> [When] all the grain is ripe, the whole town again assemble, and every man carries off the fruits of his labour, from the part [of the town field] first allotted to him, which he deposits in his own granary. . . . But previous to their carrying off their crops from the field, there is a large crib or granary, erected in the plantation, which is called the king's crib; and to this each family carries and deposits a certain quantity, according to his [*sic*] ability or inclination, or none at all if he so chooses, this in appearance seems a tribute or revenue to the mico [chief], but in fact is designed for another purpose, i.e. that of a public treasury [v. Malinowski], supplied by a few and voluntary contributions, and to which every citizen has the right of free and equal access, when his own private stores are consumed, to serve as a surplus to fly to for succour, to assist neighboring towns whose crops have failed, accommodate strangers, or travellers, afford provisions or supplies, when they go forth on hostile expeditions, and for all other exigencies of the state; and this treasure is at the disposal of the king or mico; which is surely a royal attribute to have an exclusive right and ability in a community to distribute comfort and blessings to the necessitous.[17]

In Polynesia, uses of the chiefly fund were quite similar. Chiefs provided lavish entertainments for visiting dignitaries and succored the local people in times of need. Chiefs subsidized craft production, initiated major technical works, such as irrigation projects, built temples, sponsored ceremonies, and organized support for military campaigns. The amount of goods passing

---

17 William Bartram, *The Travels of William Bartram*, Francis Harper, ed. (New Haven: Yale University Press, 1958), p. 326.

through the hands of a great Polynesian chief, and the multifarious enterprises he thus provisioned, would make a Melanesian big-man seem petty bourgeois by comparison. But then, the amount of wealth simply absorbed within the chiefly sector, just to support the elaborate administration, could cause a chiefdom to fall apart of its own weight—all of which had to be borne by the underlying population.

For in the great Polynesian chiefdoms of Hawaii or Tahiti, an interesting fraction of the chiefly fund, and much direct labor of the populace, was withheld from general circulation and instead siphoned off for the upkeep of a permanent chiefly establishment. The people's labor precipitated out as the grand houses, assembly places, and temples of chiefly precincts. It went also into sumptuary paraphernalia and the style of life to which a high chief had become accustomed, much more elegant than common folks'. This kind of conspicuous consumption, though it seems to bear out Lord Acton's appreciation of the corrupting effects of power, has a more general political significance and a more general explanation. It is awesome. It makes that symbolic contrast between ruler and ruled, disparaging to the latter as it is glorifying to the former, so conducive to a passive acceptance of authority. It is one of the more economic methods of power. Also functional, and likewise a drain on the people's resources, were the many retainers supported by a ruling chief. These were not all useless hangers-on, keepers of the royal spittoon. Many were political functionaries: supervisors of the chiefly stores, envoys to carry directives through the chiefdom, high priests intimately involved in decisions of state and the hocus-pocus by which these were communicated to the common people. Also on call were certain renowned warriors who formed a kind of praetorian guard and a body of armed executioners. If the state is a monopoly of force and the state of nature an equality of force, then the chiefdom is an intermediate condition, a majority of force, where the ruler usually has the commanding margin over any of his lesser followers. One implication among many is that a paramount chief can do with impunity unto others what others would be foolish to do unto him—like carrying off someone's daughter, or his crops.

Yet chiefly high-handedness was a dangerous game, however often Polynesian rulers were compelled to play it. Such was their contradiction. Never detached from kinship moorings, even the highest chiefs were conceived superior kinsmen to their people and morally obliged to be generous. On the other hand, chiefs were forced "to eat the powers of the government too much," as Tahitians would say: to demand beyond their just due the people's services and goods, and to convert an undue proportion of the general wealth into a swollen chiefly establishment. Funding his authority, a paramount would undermine it, and with the scepter of rule conjure the specter of rebellion.

Advanced Polynesian political systems were overtaxed. In Hawaii and other islands cycles of centralization-decentralization appear in the traditional histories: periodic violent dissolution of larger into smaller chiefdoms and, by the same means, periodic reconstitution of the great society. Sydney Parkinson accompanied Captain Cook to Polynesia and left an important account, but Northcote Parkinson would also have understood it. The expansion of a chiefdom seems to have entailed a more-than-proportionate expansion of the administrative apparatus and its conspicuous consumption. The ensuing drain on the people's wealth and expectations was eventually expressed in an unrest that destroyed both chief and chiefdom.

It has to be considered that the greater Polynesian chiefdoms—in Hawaii sometimes encompassing sections of different islands separated by leagues of open sea—were ruled, and in some measure coordinated economically, by means of communication still at the level of word-of-mouth and transportation provided only by human carriers and canoes. In these circumstances, a proliferation of administrative officials, envoys, etc., was a matter of necessity, and conspicuous consumption a hopeful economy of power. People near the "court" were most subject to its predation. The Hawaiian paramounts worried about them, and devised all manner of means to relieve the pressure on them. Not the least was a career of conquest with a view toward enlarging the tributary domain. But territorial acquisition, coupled to the increasing costs of rule, might succeed only in adding enemies abroad to those at home; and the two discontented forces were not above collusion in the time-honored practice of watering the tree of liberty with the blood of tyrants. The Hawaiians then sat cross legged upon the ground and told sad stories of the deaths of kings. "Many kings," wrote a famous custodian of Hawaiian tradition, "have been put to death by the people because of their oppression of the *makaainana* [the commoners]." [18] The object was not to overthrow the system of chieftainship but to replace a bad chief with a good one—i.e., a generous one—and reduce the burden on the *makaainana*. In this the rebellion might succeed, but perhaps only by reducing the scale of the chiefdom (thus the scale of oppression) to the nadir of the political cycle.

Like Melanesian big-man systems, the development of Polynesian chiefdoms was eventually short-circuited by an overload on the relation of chiefs to people. Still the Polynesian cut-off point was higher. Different structures have different coefficients of economic productivity and political power, as well as different limits. The comparative success of chieftainship comes of its greater impact on the household economy, its mere effective mobilization of domestic production. And the limits of chieftainship are the limits of primitive society itself. Where kinship is king, the king is in the last analysis only kinsman, and something less than royal. The same bonds that link a chief to the underlying population and give him his authority, in the end tie his hands.

This parochial comparison of Pacific Island societies can be put to the service of another general point: chiefdom formation alters the social profile of exchange, the incidence of different modes of reciprocity, just as segmentary tribes introduce changes in this respect by comparison with hunting bands.

In the isolated camps of marginal food collectors, the uncertainties of the chase are mitigated by a collective emphasis on share and share alike. "Their culture insists that they share with each other, and it has never happened that a Bushman failed to share objects, food or water with other members of his band, for without very rigid co-operation Bushmen could not survive the famines and droughts the Kalahari offers them." [19] This demand of co-opera-

---

[18] David Malo, *Hawaiian Antiquities* (Honolulu: Hawaiian Gazette Co., 1903), p. 258.
[19] Elizabeth Marshall Thomas, *The Harmless People* (New York: Knopf, 1959), p. 22; see also Service, *op. cit.*

tion, combined with but few opportunities of direct trade with outsiders, puts generalized reciprocity in the position of the dominant mode of exchange.

By contrast, the social horizons of tribesmen are usually broader, the range of their transactions wider, and the balanced reciprocity enjoined in the world beyond competes now with homebred generosity for importance in the tribal scheme of things. To the local organization of band society the segmentary tribe adds new dimensions of peripheral structure, and to local exchange new economic relations in the intercommunity and inter-tribal sectors. Development takes place precisely in the areas where balanced exchange is appropriate, whether in pursuit of goods from a distance or of peace and alliance with other communities. By comparison with bands, segmentary tribes show an increase, greater or less in different circumstances, in the proportion of balanced to generalized exchange. In the line of this development, perhaps the most complete expression of it, is the appearance of "primitive money" in some tribal regions; e.g., the shell currencies of Melanesia and aboriginal California. Functioning as customary standards of equivalence and media of exchange, these monies both reflect and facilitate a heavy balanced traffic.[20] Not all segmentary tribes have money, but tribes that have money are typically segmentary tribes. Primitive money is rare or nonexistent in the less developed band economies. And also in the more developed chiefdoms—however much that goes against our own views of economic progress.

But in the chiefdom the internal economy regains predominance over the external, partly by a process of sheer displacement. The progression from segmentary tribe to chiefdom is in one sense a transformation of external into internal relations, as adjacent local groups are integrated under the aegis of powerful chiefs and (often) extensive descent groups. Balanced reciprocity falls off in consequence. Its incidence is restricted, first, by the "internalization" of exchange relationships; the drawing-together of people in major political and descent associations tend to generalize reciprocity between them. Second, it is restricted by the prevalence of rank. Rank becomes a factor in the calculus of almost every transaction, imposing elements of imbalance out of considerations of status. Third and most significant is the centralization of exchange in a public economy. Reciprocities focus on the ruling chiefs, to whom all must give their due and from whom flow "comforts and blessings to the necessitous." Thus integrated politically, reciprocity changes in quality. It reappears in a higher form, the collective pooling and reallocation of goods by powers-that-be, a process deserving its own name—*redistribution.*

Malinowski saw in the chief's accumulation and disbursement of goods, ". . . the prototype of the public finance system and the organization of State treasuries of to-day." The prototype, however, has its own prototypes, not only in the chiefdom itself but at all stages of primitive society. Redistribution—in this form it is also known as "pooling" and "householding"—is what families do everywhere, their individual members contributing to the common

---

[20] They are especially useful where seasonal differences in production render difficult the direct exchange of local commodities. But it should be cautioned I use "primitive money" in a restricted sense: goods primarily of exchange-value rather than inherent use-value and employed (in peripheral sectors) as means of exchange against a variety of other goods— whatever else their purpose. For a broader conception of "money" and its distribution, see George Dalton, "Primitive Money," *American Anthropologist*, LXVII (1965), 44–65.

hearth and receiving therefrom a due share. It is ordinary practice as well in connection with cooperative food production, such as impounding buffalo in the northern Plains or net fishing in a Polynesian lagoon, where the catch is collected and then divided among all participants. Chiefly redistribution must derive some of its political efficacy by analogy with these more humble forms, but even more from the fact that this integration of reciprocities changes the whole sociology of exchange. In its simpler form, reciprocity is a *between* relation, the action and response of two parties. Although the exchange may establish harmony between them, the differentiation of parties, the distinction of interests, is here inescapable. But where reciprocity separates, redistribution combines. Redistribution is a *within* relation, the collective action of a group, and of a group, moreover, with a social center where goods are concentrated and thence flow outward. Redistribution is chieftainship said in economics.

Six Tribal Religion

When we were pastoral nomads, the Lord was our shepherd. We were His flock, and He made us to lie down in green pastures, and led us beside the still waters.

When we were serfs and nobles, the Lord was our king. Sat regnant on the throne of heaven, His shepherd's crook now a jeweled scepter: monarch of feudal monarchs, even to a Prince of Evil, His own contentious baron. But we were mostly peasants, and our comfort and justice no longer lay in the green pastures but in the land. And we would have it. We would inherit the earth.

Finally we are businessmen—and the Lord is our accountant. He keeps a ledger on us all, enters there our good deeds in black and debits our sins in red. The Lord useth double-entry bookkeeping; He writeth a man down in fine columns. And when the Great Businessman closes our accounts, to those who show a profit He shall pay eternal dividends; but for those with a life ill spent —well, the Devil take the hindmost.

It is too facile to say that man created God (or gods) in his own image.

"God is another name for society." The view of the famous Durkheim, thus metaphorically compressed, remains one of two prevailing anthropological perspectives on religion. In the divine, men realize to themselves the moral authority of society, the discipline beyond themselves to which they submit, which constrains their behavior even in spite of themselves, contradicts their impulses, rewards their compliance, and so renders them dependent and grateful for it:

> Since it is in spiritual ways that social pressure exercises itself, it could not fail to give men the idea that outside themselves there exist one or several powers, both moral and, at the same time, efficacious, upon which they depend. They must think of these powers, at least in part, as outside themselves, for these address them in a tone of command and sometimes even order them to do violence to their most natural inclinations. It is undoubtedly true that if they were able to see that these influences which they feel emanate from society, then the mythological system of interpretations would never be born. But social action follows ways that are too circuitous and obscure. . . . As long as scientific analysis does not come to teach it to them, men know well that they are acted upon, but they do not know by whom. So they must invent by themselves the idea of these powers with which they feel themselves in connection, and from that, we are able to catch a glimpse of the way by which they were led to represent them under forms that are really foreign to their nature and to transfigure them by thought.[1]

By the spirits, men represent the secular forces under which they live, and in the rituals of religious cult, where the power of society is materialized in the collectivity of worshippers, they affirm their dependence upon this power —which is to say, they affirm the authority of society as constituted. From this follow several corollary propositions repeatedly met in modern anthropology: that spiritual beliefs mirror the structure of society; that gods, myths, and ritual practices symbolize the main social values and relationships; that all these function to integrate society, provide cohesion, promote solidarity, and maintain continuity.

But God is also another name for technology—or, it may be, for economics or politics. This is the second of the two main anthropological theses on religion. It was adumbrated at length by Malinowski, but particularly in reference to magic, technical processes, and Trobriand Islanders. Magic, Malinowski suggested, steps in where the technical issue is beyond ordinary human competence and control, where the uncertain productive procedure involves serious risks to life and livelihood. The native's experience has taught him, Malinowski wrote,

> . . . that in spite of all his forethought and beyond all his efforts there are agencies and forces which one year bestow unwonted and unearned benefits of fertility, making everything run smooth and well, rain and sun appear at the right moment, noxious insects remain in abeyance, the harvest yields a superabundant crop; and another year again the same agencies bring ill luck and bad chance, pursue him from beginning till end and thwart all his most strenuous efforts and his best-founded knowledge. To control these influences and these only he employs magic.[2]

---

[1] Emile Durkheim, *The Elementary Forms of the Religious Life* (Glencoe, Ill.: The Free Press, 1947), p. 209.

[2] Bronislaw Malinowski, *Magic, Science and Religion* (New York: Doubleday Anchor Books, 1954), pp. 28–29.

Malinowski went on to exemplify, adducing a now-famous contrast between the ritual accompaniments of Trobriand fishing in the inner lagoon ("done in an easy and absolutely reliable manner") and the dangerous angling of the open sea. In connection with the former, "where man can rely completely upon his skill and knowledge," there is no magic; but for the latter, "full of danger and uncertainty," magic is extensive.

I think it safe to generalize Malinowski's thesis from magic to a variety of religious practices and beliefs, and also from technical practice to the economic and social order. Malinowski himself, in discussing certain religious rites— which he distinguished from magic—invoked a similar explanation of their incidence and function, that they entered at a moment of social crisis and acted to resolve it. The general thesis would read then like this: the super-natural dream-stuff comes into play, in conception or action (ritual), at points of stress in the economic and social order, where ordinary procedures and arrangements are insufficient to sustain the system. Supernaturalism can be expected in connection with economic uncertainty, whether occasioned by inadequate technical means or untoward natural events. It acts to blunt con-tradictions and conflicts of interest in existing social relations. It collaborates with politics at the latter's points of weakness, to buttress authority, conse-crate peace, or mobilize war. Cultures, I repeat, find gods in foxholes. Where normal economic and political means fail, supernatural reserves are thrown into the breach and take over the defense.

From this societal function, the individual "thumb-sucking" function of religion is clearly derivative. In the course of its general duties, or as one aspect of them, religion may quiet personal fears, instill confidence, and encourage one generally to carry on. At certain times in a person's life it comforts him to know he shall see his ancestors after death—and it enables society's work to be done. But it may be as necessary for the latter objective to cause fear and promote anxiety, which religious beliefs and rituals are also known to do. That sinners burn in hell is no comfort to those who harbor evil impulses, and the anguish of the thought may be just enough to repress the impulse— and enable society's work to be done. After all, we are taught both to love God and to fear Him.

On religion's defense of society, Malinowski's and Durkheim's theories come into tangent. Otherwise they tend to be complementary. Durkheim speaks mainly to the content of religion, Malinowski to the incidence. Pro-jecting from Malinowski's view, it should follow that different societies de-velop different quotients of supernaturalism, depending on the difficulties with which they are beset. Tribesmen are often quite religious, but they are not necessarily full time servants of mumbojumbo. Some are decidedly uncon-cerned about it.

It follows also from Malinowskian principles that the role of supernatural-ism in relation to other cultural spheres and activities will vary from tribe to tribe. Here an intensive ritual is conjoined with technical processes, there a domestic ghost cult is the main preoccupation, in a third place religion is village politics by other means.

To say these approaches to religion, Durkheim's and Malinowski's, are complementary—and seemingly exhaustive of the problems—is not to say they are completely satisfactory. Of course, I have oversimplified them, but even the originals have been subject to repeated criticism. They seem to belong to that category of ideas that are too true to be good, but by the same quality impossible to forget—so in the more substantive discussion of tribal religion to follow, the student will detect at many points a visitation by one or the other of two great ancestral spirits.

The Supernatural
as a Segmentary System

The objective of this section is to relate tribal conceptions of spiritual beings to the tribal segmentary design.

The Nuer [3] divide the spirits into "spirits of the above" and "spirits of the below." Spirits of the above include the Supreme Spirit (*Kwoth*, or *Kwoth a nhial*, "Spirit who is in the sky"), spirits of the air, and *col wic*, souls of people killed by lightning. Spirits of the below are totemic spirits, nature sprites, and the forces residing in fetish-objects. (There are also ghosts, but they are not included in this classification, nor given much attention by the Nuer.)

The Nuer, Evans-Pritchard observes, comprehend the many spirits also as the One: all other being so many manifestations ("refractions") of the great *Kwoth*. The others are *Kwoth* in different contexts, especially as figured in relation to social entities of different order in the tribal hierarchy. *Kwoth* is "God," spirit in relation to mankind (that is to say, divinity at the tribal level). But just as different European towns have their own tutelary Madonnas, so greater and lesser segments of the tribe have their own patron versions of *Kwoth*—in several categorical forms, as are appropriate to the constitution and functions of the several social groups. Spirits of the air are guardians of the prophets who unite large political confederations, thus derivatively they are patrons of these political bodies.[4] The *col wic* are spirits of the lineages and families to which they belonged in life—or *Kwoth* in relation to these groups—and the totemic spirits likewise mainly patrons of lineages. Nature sprites relate to families and individuals in their private capacities, and fetishes are also tutelaries of individuals. (While the different spiritual classes represent segments of different order, or *Kwoth* in relation to segments of different order, it is possible also to appeal directly to more comprehensive spirits, and notably for persons to appeal directly to *Kwoth*.)

The Nuer have a segmentary lineage system. Their conception of the One in the many is consistent with the logic of such a system:

> Given the segmentary political and lineage system of the Nuer it is understandable that the same complementary tendencies toward fission and fusion and the same relativity that we find in the structure are found also in the action of Spirit in the social life. Just as, for example, two

---

[3] A general account of Nuer religion, which figures heavily in this section, may be found in E. E. Evans-Pritchard, *Nuer Religion* (Oxford: Clarendon Press, 1956). A summary of sociological aspects of Nuer religion appears in Evans-Pritchard, "The Nuer Conception of Spirit in Its Relation to the Social Order," *American Anthropologist*, LV (1953), 201–214.

[4] The prophets and the confederations of local groups they mobilize are modern developments, apparently in response to recent Arab and European intrusions.

lineages are distinct and opposed groups in relation to one another at one level of segmentation and are a single unit at a higher level of segmentation, so Spirit as conceived in relation to these segments must be divided at the lower level and undivided at the higher level. It is intelligible, therefore, that in its relation to the segmentary social order the conception of Spirit is broken up into diverse refractions, while in relation to nature and man in general the many become again the one.[5]

It may be that this figuration of one Spirit in several representations is singularly appropriate to a segmentary lineage system, itself harmonious in principle from top to bottom and materializing at various levels by "complementary opposition." But some correlation of distinct spirit-beings or supernatural forces with distinct levels of the segmentary hierarchy is quite general among tribesmen, whether or not the tutelaries of the lower social orders are the Divine otherwise and parochially conceived. The different categories of spirit are also commonly in some relation of rank and perhaps descent, again if not of ultimate identity.

The Mae Enga of the New Guinea Highlands exist as a people under a great tribe of Sky People, who in a general and final-analysis way, and with an Olympian indifference to human wish, control man's fate.[6] The Sky People are descendants of the sun and moon, "the father and mother of us all." Feuding, raising pigs, and growing crops, organized in patrilineal groups, the Sky People live above exactly as do the Enga below; and as each Enga phratry was established by a member of an homologous Sky Phratry, the structure of Sky-People society duplicates the structure of Enga-people society. Thus in an unusually precise way God [7] is indeed another name for society. Then, below the level of Enga society-as-a-whole, there are two segments of especial importance, the territorially based clans and the families, and to these and their particular concerns correspond other supernatural types. Each clan has its collective body of remote ancestors—descendants of the clan founder, himself descended from a Sky-Person phratry founder—who are placated in the event of clan-wide misfortune. Families as such deal with powerful domestic ghosts, spirits of the recently departed. Besides, solitary travelers in the high mountain bush may have personal encounters with demons who intend them no good. Individual men also possess magical spells, derived from originals in the possession of the clan founder, which are used mainly for private purposes.

The different categories of spirit in a tribal pantheon have usually distinct segmentary status. At the same time, each type of supernatural has particular attributes, powers, functions, a rank or valuation in the divine order involving implicit or express relationships to other types, a station in the cosmos, and a

---

[5] Evans-Pritchard, *Nuer Religion*, p. 115.

[6] Mervyn Meggitt, "The Mae Enga of the Western Highlands," in P. Lawrence and M. Meggitt, eds., *Gods, Ghosts and Men in Melanesia* (Melbourne: Oxford University Press, 1965), pp. 105–131.

[7] But notice by comparison with the Nuer the decentralized character of Enga higher-level Divinity. The difference corresponds to structural contrasts between these otherwise quite similar societies. The Nuer, crystallizing large (if relative) lineage formations through complementary opposition, are by their segmentary system more extensively united than the Enga. Nor are the Enga as a people, an ethnic entity, as well-delineated as the Nuer.

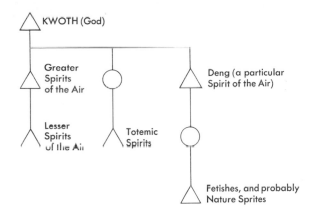

Figure 6.1. Genealogy of Nuer spirit-classes.

corresponding cult of its devotees. The point the following discussion seeks to document is that in these several respects, the qualities of a spirit-being are consistent with its segmentary status, with its social order.

Back in the upper paleolithic of the book, in Chapter 2, I proposed that the tribal segmentary scheme be viewed from two vantages: as a hierarchy of progressively inclusive groups, and as a series of increasingly broad spheres of co-membership—in other words, a system of augmenting order and widening scope, of height and breadth, plane and universality. Here I argue that the same system is more or less faithfully projected onto the spiritual domain, to give cosmic attribute and dimension to supernatural beings. The higher the social order in relation to which spiritual forces figure, the higher their rank in the order of divinity, and perhaps literally the higher their position in the cosmos. The broader the social sector in relation to which spiritual forces figure, the greater their extension or sphere of immanence.[8]

Consider the status system of the gods. The spirits of higher-order groups are Higher Powers. A lineage people, the Nuer use a genealogical idiom to express relationships between different categories of spirit (Fig. 6.1). In a way then totally unsubtle, patrilineal values are enlisted to make invidious distinctions of divine grade. *Kwoth*, the tribal god and indeed creator of the universe, is the genealogical source. Greater spirits of the air are children of *Kwoth*, and lesser spirits of the air, children of *Kwoth*'s sons. Thus all spirits of the above—that is to say, patrons of the greater social bodies—are members of God's lineage. Within the lineage they are ranked by generational seniority, by filial status. But all spirits of the below descend from females of God's line, a patrilineal way of devaluing them: they are not in God's lineage, or they are accessory branches of God's lineage. And as children of *Kwoth*'s daughters and granddaughters, respectively, totemic sprites and fetishes are apparently progressively depreciated by generational remove. The description of Enga spiritdom (above) harbors a similar, though simpler, genealogy.

With their distinction between spirits of the above and spirits of the below,

---

[8] Evans-Pritchard observes that Nuer spirits decrease in number but increase in permanence or stability in proportion to spiritual grade. Spirits of the lowest categories tend to be more numerous and shorter-lived than higher spirits. Such variations seem generally relevant to a segmentary design and generally the case in tribal religions. The variation in number of members of spirit-categories parallels the decrease in number of units at each ascending level of the segmentary pyramid. The higher-order social bodies also tend to be more permanent than their component segments.

and the finer vertical gradations within each class, corresponding generally to successive levels of the social hierarchy, the Nuer also provide a first-class illustration of a relation between cosmic height and segmentary level, a neater example perhaps than is ordinarily encountered. The supernatural representations of higher-order social groups are literally "on high," the others ranged accordingly on a scale of heaven and earth. *Kwoth* is symbolized by the sky and associated with major celestial bodies. Spirits of the air are of the atmosphere, clouds and breezes, the greater of them closer to God and the lesser nearer to earth; whereas, at the "lower" extreme, some fetishes speak from below the ground.

The installation of the tribal-level Divinity in the heavenly sphere happens to be a very widespread practice—as witness the Sky People of the Enga, Sun of the Crow Indians, and Great Spirit of the Iroquois, whose abode is in heaven.[9] But, of course, not only among tribesmen.

I hasten to add that a direct transposition of the segmentary scheme onto the universe, resulting in a simple linear progression from earthbound lesser spirits and forces to celestial gods, is not general or even normal tribal cosmology, and to suppose so would leave one ill-prepared to cope with the metaphysical subtleties tribesmen frequently concoct for the mystification of anthropologists. The symbolic opposition of heaven and earth is common enough, but usually in connection with a systematic dualism involving also correlated oppositions of male and female, life and death, day and night, right and left, etc. Spirit-categories are in various ways integrated into the dualistic frame, perhaps bisected by it, such that the high gods themselves are divided according to sex between heaven and earth. In the Polynesian beginning the Sky Father cohabited with the Earth Mother, and they remained in that position until one of their divine offspring (in a fit of oedipal pique) managed to pry them apart and make room for Polynesia. In another widespread permutation, an underworld of the dead is added to the planes of heaven and earth. This three-tiered universe is the combined logical product of three dualisms: above and below, divine and mortal, life and death. As mortal, man is below the gods, but as alive, he is above the dead; hence the three spheres— divines above, mortals on earth, and shades below. Matters become truly complicated when the dead are also divine, as are the Hopi Indians' ancestors (*kachinas*). Then, if as dead the ancestors are below, still as spirits they are above—the *kachinas* are also clouds. The Hopi underworld is in fact a precise antithesis of the world above and is linked to the world above by a continuous passage of beings back and forth, and an endless cycle of birth, death, and regeneration. Sun, rising from the underworld in the east, descends in the west to complete its circle below, so that when it is day in the pueblo of the living it is night in the pueblo of the dead, and our night is their day; and the ancestors are clouds, under Sun, who bring rain to the living, and so at the winter solstice ascend to dwell among the living, to return below at the summer solstice; and when a man dies he is washed as a baby to be reborn among the dead, and when a baby is born among the living it is the soul of one dead returned to the company of the quick.[10] Remarkably enough, Nuer

---

[9] The cult of the Eearth in West Africa seems a major exception.

[10] Mischa Titiev, *Old Oraibi*, Papers of the Peabody Museum of American Archaeology and Ethnology, Harvard University, XXII (1944).

belief duplicates this Hopi cosmology in fundamental respects. The Nuer propound many of the same dualisms, as well as an inchoate notion of an underworld of the dead and some conception of ghostly power.[11] Yet ancestor-worship is as it were repressed among the Nuer—for reasons that may become clear in the following section [12]—and the cosmos accordingly is foreshortened below, leaving only the linear progression of spirit from earth to heaven.

Spirit has scope as well as rank and height. It is manifest in phenomena of greater or less local extent, and concerned functionally with human affairs of greater or less generality. This sphere of its immanence and influence is commensurate with the compass of the social group with which the spirit is associated. I advert here to the tribe in its sectoral dimension, and to spirit in its property of extension.

A god is where its people is. Tribal high gods are as extensive as the tribe; they are pervasive, universal gods. They are manifest in the things that happen to everyone, responsible in some way for customs and morals of general practice and observation. In a society such as Nuer, all this is spiritually centralized, in God, and what is less than this is decentralized, in other spirits:

> Mighty and celestial phenomena and great and terrible happenings, such as plagues and famines, and the moral order which concern all men are attributed to God [*Kwoth*], while processes and events which do not have so general a range of impact tend to be attributed to whichever particular refraction or type of refraction the situation and context evoke.[13]

Mysterious are the great gods: unrestricted in location, manifold in expression. But lesser spirits and forces, of smaller social scope, are accordingly limited in manifestation. Their locus is more definite, their shape more specific. Diminishing in social impact, they are increasingly bound to certain material forms, identified in certain emanations. These forms vary in generality of definition according to the generality of the social group they represent. Totems of clans or lineages are usually natural *species:* bear, ostrich, tree-fern. A species is a class of things, composed of individual members of like qualities, as a clan is a class of like people. But the power of a personal fetish or amulet resides entirely in the particular object, as also the sorcerer's magic is bound up in the spell. Supernatural forces generally increase in materiality and particularity as they decrease in social range. And at some point in this social regression there usually appears a transition from natural forms to cultural— or from natural to human to cultural. The least of spiritual things are man-made. They become by that token less spiritual. They are manipulated as the gods cannot be manipulated; they are put to man's bidding as only God could put man to His. All over the tribal world fetishes and spells are bought and sold. Again no one sells God, although it is said some try to buy Him by sacrifice.

If God is everywhere, then He is nowhere in particular and nothing does to describe Him. Less bound to specific material forms, tribal great spirits are often accordingly difficult to define, to specify as to properties and qualities

---

11 Evans-Pritchard, *Nuer Religion.*
12 See below, p. 107.
13 Evans-Pritchard, *op. cit.,* p. 211.

other than "good," "all-knowing," "eternal," and the like. The tribal Supreme Spirit, if there is one, is a particularly difficult case—"pure spirit," as Evans-Pritchard says, ineffable. For some reason, it almost never fails to astonish anthropologists that the people are unable to give a coherent description of their tribal High God, although why they any more than Christians should be able to do so is difficult to say. In any event, the incomprehensibility of the Supreme Being is a common phenomenon among tribesmen who have one. For instance,

> The Sun, to be sure, means more to a greater number of persons [among Crow Indians] then any one other spirit; he approaches more nearly than any other our notion of a Supreme Being. Yet what astonishing conceptions cluster about him, and in what chaos is Crow theology concerning the most elementary definition of his identity! The most trustworthy witnesses cannot agree as to whether he is identical with Old-Man-Coyote, the hero of Crow folklore; nay, in a single cosmogonic myth there is constant vacillation on this point.[14]

But then, the Supreme Being often doesn't do much—or at least what has he done lately? I mentioned that the functional concern of a spirit-being in human affairs is related to its sectoral scope, such that the highest gods are linked to general cultural interests and common values, and perhaps to the collective activities of large groups, even as lineage and family spirits watch over the affairs of these segments while fetishes and spells are usually put to private purposes. In this connection, major tribal gods—but ordinarily not the Supreme Spirit, if one exists—are allotted special cultural provinces within the general domain: one may be the god of war, another of crops, a third of hunting, another of rain, etc. (So different Nuer spirits of the air are associated with sickness, cattle plague, rain and lightning, war, and rivers and streams.) Tribal labors are divided among various *department gods*. Now, a Supreme Being may be in some sense supreme over all these activities, which is to say over all common human affairs, yet exercise very little influence in anything. It is not that there is little left for Him to do; the same impotence may attend all the high gods, despite their presumed competences. The point is that on the seventh day God did not simply rest—He retired altogether.

That Nuer address simpler prayers to *Kwoth* makes Him blessed even among the gods. Many tribal Great Spirits, perhaps the majority of them, are technically described as *otiose*. As Supreme Beings they are supremely indifferent to human beings, without the slightest inclination to intervene in people's latest troubles. Distant beyond call, God is put in the past tense: the Great Spirit came first and created the world, after which He went away. The Mende of Sierra Leone explain that He took refuge high in the sky after creating people, for fear of being worn out by their constant requests. Perhaps God will be credited with a little more: perhaps He controls man's fate in an ultimate way, or perhaps indirectly through lesser spirits whose powers come of Him; and from here one moves by insensible gradations to a Nuer *Kwoth*, or beyond. But frequently God is no more than a *culture-hero*, a status He may even have to share with lesser gods. That is, He figures as a first cause, an

---

[14] Robert H. Lowie, *Primitive Religion* (New York: Liveright, 1948), p. 21.

explanation of the origin of important things such as the earth, people, crops, tribal customs. God did it. His present existence then is confined to myth. In the language of the Ngaing of New Guinea, the name of the Supreme Being is the word for "myth." As reported by the ethnographer Peter Lawrence, this Myth is a fair average otiose God:

> . . . when asked how their world began, the people reply: 'Parambik put (*riring*) everything.' By this they mean that Parambik 'put' the earth, bush, mountains, rivers, wild animals, birds and plants (including the totems), and the war gods in the bush areas. . . . Parambik is described as a god (*tut*) but, unlike the other deities, is said to be very remote. He is all-pervasive and has no fixed sanctuary. Even his name is merely the general word for myth. Although held responsible for the primary elements of the Ngaing cosmos, he is not thought to take further interest in it and no ritual is performed in association with him.[15]

Thus a discrepancy appears between spiritual scope and spiritual power. Parambik is "all-pervasive," but ineffectual, ineffectual in the sense that an explanation is no solution. If a god's cosmic domain is commensurate with his social compass, still his existential authority need not grow in proportion. As Lawrence suggests, a spirit's current efficacy is measurable by the ritual devoted to him. In turn, the cults of spirits of different order vary (and in complicated ways) with the character of the segmentary scheme. To these relations between cult, spiritual power, and the tribal design we now turn.

Cults

The vitality and imminence of God, or of the several high gods or of any other class of spirit, depends on whether "he is a god for the day when a god is needed," as the Hawaiians would say. It is a question of invocation and supplication, of the cult and ritual fuss made over him. God pays as much attention to people as people do to Him. The otiose Supreme Being is a derivative of a common segmentary calculus of cultish practice—*viz.*, ritual intensity is inversely related to spiritual supremacy. Even among the Nuer,

> . . . the lower down the scale of spirit we descend the more prominent do cultic features appear. God is approached in simple prayer and sacrifice. The spirits of the air receive more elaborate ceremonial attentions, into which enter hymns, possession, and divination. Cultic features are also prominent at the level of *col wic* and totemic spirits. The most regular ritual attention appears to be given to the fetishes, which receive frequent offerings from their owners and in the most material form.[16]

A ritual maximization of minimal spirits seems logical in the light of a segmentary tribal design, and notably expectable among decentralized, seg-

---

[15] Peter Lawrence, "The Ngaing of the Rai Coast," in *Gods, Ghosts and Men in Melanesia*, pp. 203–204.
[16] Evans-Pritchard, "The Nuer Conception of Spirit in Relation to The Social Order," 212.

mentary tribes proper. Without insisting on a strictly progressive increase in the ritual attentions afforded lesser spirits, it is at least likely that the most prominent cults will concern spirits of some lower social level, such as the personal or the familial, and the tribal religion will thus appear predominantly a ghost cult, ancestor worship, fetish worship or a prevalence of witches. In the decentralized tribe, higher levels of the organization are progressively reduced in function, incoherent, and ill-defined. The weight of culture is carried on the lower levels, the stresses are greatest in the inner circles, the need of solidarity perhaps more essential and certainly more continuous at the infrastructure, the economic risks taken here, and here where pots crack, fish won't bite, women go bad and kids die—in short, this is where the action is, and the problems. This is where the main cult is.

The main cult of the Enga concerns domestic ghosts. The great Sky People are not wholly detached from human affairs, but they are totally beyond human reach. Up there, living the life of Enga, they control the weather. They decide on rain. They stoke up their house fires and the smoke becomes clouds that cover the sun. They call out in loud voices—thus, thunder. They open their doors and flames from their fires shoot out—lightning. The lightning tears holes in the clouds, through which the Sky People urinate— rain. Such is the gods' relation to men. And when it so rains on the Enga— they let it rain. The Sky People have their own reasons, and cannot be supplicated, placated, or otherwise ritually approached. It is not then surprising, as Mervyn Meggitt observes, ". . . that they enter little into peoples' calculations. . . . They are rarely mentioned."

By contrast, ". . . not a day passes but someone refers publicly to the activities of ghosts." [17] Domestic ghosts are responsible for almost all personal misfortune of consequence: for injury, illness, and death. If a man is ill or seriously hurt, close relatives kill a pig to placate the ghost presumed responsible: the ghost consumes the essence of the cooking pig and the blood; the relatives get the meat. If the sufferer does not then recover, a diviner is consulted to determine the correct ghost, or the correct number of pigs to kill—and one can lose a fair lot of pigs that way, not to mention a relative. Should misfortune dog a whole clan—e.g., a general crop failure or illness approaching epidemic proportions—the body of clan ancestral ghosts is propitiated in a more elaborate collective rite. (This involves, among other things, services of a ritual expert presiding over ceremonies in a clan cult house, exhumation of certain stones from which the ancestors' power emanates, killing of pigs to the ancestors, and certain exchanges with neighboring clans.) The body of clan ghosts collectively conceived is the highest class of supernatural ritually contacted by the Enga, but perhaps not until domestic rites devoted to particular ghosts have failed to stem the tide of misfortune and it mounts to flood stage.

The Enga cults of collective clan ancestors and particular domestic ghosts represent two of several different conceptions appearing indiscriminately in the anthropological record under the general head of "ancestor worship." In turn, ancestor worship is often broadly reckoned the appropriate theology of a lineage system, or at least of lineal inheritance and succession rights on the domestic level. Death is not the end and, to transpose a Faulknerism from the

---

[17] M. Meggitt, in *Gods, Ghosts and Men in Melanesia*, p. 109.

South to the lineage, the past is not dead—it is not even past. The existing arrangements of a lineage, its divisions and further subdivisions, the rights of various members, segments, and of the whole *vis-a-vis* other lineages, are the present residue of past history, of who begat and did otherwise to whom. The dead survive in the relationships of the living. In its whole and in its parts, the lineage is thus explained by invocation of the ancestors and it is so validated. In secular contexts we have the genealogy, which as Malinowski taught, is the "charter" of the lineage, the warrant for its present constitution and the privileges of its members. The mystical analogue of the genealogy is ancestor worship. Here the responsibility of the dead for the condition of the living is expressed in the notion that the lineage includes dead as well as living, that they are still with us, that they continue to influence our lives. Ancestor worship is a supernatural representation of a social fact.

Ancestor worship is appropriate to lineage organization but not its inevitable concomitant. Some noted examples of lineage sociology do not apotheosize their forebears, however much the ancestors are invoked in genealogical mode to rationalize existing arrangements. This is true of Nuer, and also Tiv. With their segmentary lineage systems, one might expect of these peoples a veritable segmentary hierarchy of ancestor worship: shrines and rituals devoted to the founder at each successive level of integration. Such parallel hierarchies of lineage segment and tutelary ancestor exist, as among the Tallensi of Nigeria, and something of the sort appears in connection with conical clan organization in Polynesia. But not among the Tiv or Nuer. Both believe in ghosts, yet these are effectively removed from the human sphere at the termination of the mourning period, consigned to another place or form, without any further effect as spirits-of-the-departed upon their descendants. On the other hand, the crystallization of higher-order lineages argued by autonomous ancestor cults would be inconsistent with the functioning of Tiv-Nuer segmentary lineage systems. Recall that as political entities, lineages above the minimum level do not exist as such or function autonomously, but emerge only in opposition to like units and as the order of opposition dictates. In fixing this complementary opposition, a hierarchy of ancestor cults would destroy its flexibility.

In the domestic ghost cult of the Enga, the spirits of the fathers return to plague the sons. Other familiar shades may also be offensive, but Enga say, " 'The ghost of my father's father killed my father and my father's ghost will kill me!' " [18] These fond sentiments of filial regard invite interpretation on lines similar to lineage ancestor-worship—*viz.*, the continuation of parental authority after death. Visiting punishment on his offspring, a father manifests in death the same power he held in life; ritually propitiating the old man's ghost, the son shows the same submission. Ghosthood is the relation between father and son spiritually metamorphosed.

But the life-relationship thus transfigured is characteristically complex, involving conflict as well as compliance—not to mention love—and on this point further interpretations of cults of the recently dead have turned.[19] In a patri-

---

[18] Meggitt, *op. cit.*, 112.

[19] I rely heavily on Fortes' analysis of Tallensi ancestor worship. Meyer Fortes, "Pietas in Ancestor Worship," *The Journal of the Royal Anthropological Institute*, LIXI (1960), 166–191.

archal household, the son would replace him whom he must obey, for he is heir as well as subject to his father's authority. Between fathers and sons there is a conflict of interest and an ineluctable tension, even as the competition is ordinarily suppressed by amity, duty, and dependence. Thus in life and in death fatherhood evokes an ambivalent compound of antagonism and filial piety, dread and reverence, but often in different measures in different societies. The dead are more positively or more negatively conceived. So the ethnographer of the Tallensi (Fortes) speaks of "ancestors" where the ethnographer of the Enga (Meggitt) sees only "ghosts." Different kinds of interpretation are accordingly suggested. Vengeance apotheosized, the Enga domestic ghost cult seems directly explicable from the aspect of conflict.[20] For the ghost is only neutral when he is not malevolent, as if his death meant above all his dispossession. But the Tallensi parental spirit is a guardian and revered even for his (just) power. Here a dialectic conclusion appears appropriate: that filial piety, accommodating the son to the coercive authority of the father in life and after death, resolves or at least mitigates the contradiction between their conflict and their love.[21]

A difference of this character—i.e., between pious reverence for the dead and mere dread of them—may be further related to the role of ancestral spirits as sanction of their descendants' morality. The ancestors' concern with peoples' misdeeds varies widely. In some tribes, the people must contend with an indiscriminate ghostly malevolence, to which human conduct whether good or bad is irrelevant; elsewhere, they must account to a just ancestral power, certain to visit harm on descendants for violating moral relations with kinsmen (or pious relations with ancestors). Where some tribesmen are just unlucky, others sin. It is not this difference, however, but a commonality I should like to emphasize: that the dead, and characteristically the recently dead, are responsible for people's personal misfortunes, their sicknesses, the failures of their well-laid plans, their deaths. By that token relief becomes humanly possible—through rituals of expiation, propitiation, or the laying of ghosts. The dead thus operate on the personal level of religion, as cause and cure of personal tragedy.

The dead are not unique in this capacity; there exist functional analogues, notably sorcerers and witches. If the Tallensi or the Enga put the blame on ancestors or ghosts, the Dobuans or the Azande allege that human agencies are responsible for a person's troubles. The contrast may be even more severe than blaming the dead versus impugning the living. More fundamentally it may be a difference between blame directed inward in light of one's own guilt, as where ancestors are believed to visit harm for moral transgressions, and blame directed onto others in light of their evil intent, as in charges of witchcraft or sorcery laid against fellow tribesmen. Take into account certain Afri-

---

[20] Meggitt thus accommodates the offensiveness of ghosts other than the father, notably of siblings, by reference to the tensions and rivalries of Enga family life.

[21] A sufficient explanation of the difference between revered ancestors and feared ghosts as exemplified here by Tallensi and Enga would probably have to consider the larger lineage and ancestor-cult contexts. Of more immediate relevance, the jural minority of the Tallensi son seems more prolonged, not finished until the father's death; hence, the intergenerational conflict is intense and a major problem in the system.

can notions of witchcraft and practically the complete range of mystic responses to personal misfortune is presented. At one extreme, it is your own fault punished by ancestors who do not exist; at the opposed extreme, it is the design of others, inflicted by witches who do not exist.[22]

For witches need be no more substantial than ancestors. To understand this, it is necessary to distinguish witchcraft from sorcery, with which the former is often confused. Many African peoples themselves make just such a distinction, and in such a way as to convey the suspicion that witches are entirely illusory. Witches are inherently evil, their black powers perhaps inherited but in any event part of their makeup, their organic constitution, even demonstrable upon autopsy as an unusual growth (a "witchcraft substance") upon the heart, the liver, or it may be the gall bladder. And witches' powers are psychic: their souls fly through the night to eat people, feeding on the soul-stuff of hapless victims. Sorcerers come in many varieties. Some practice bad (black) magic and some good (white). But even if evil-intentioned, they are humanly so. Their powers are learned, usually from some other sorcerer, and reside not in themselves but in the "medicines" they manipulate or in spells they recite. The distinction is important because sorcerers are often "real" but witches are not. That is, sorcerers have been known to practice, yet I think no anthropologist has actually witnessed witchcraft. Witch beliefs, so far as one keen student is concerned, are "the standardized nightmare of the group."[23] Plainly, they are projections of hostility along lines of tension in the social structure. Witches are people who hate you. Or is it vice versa? At any rate, the thought is father to the witch.[24]

A question always arises about the mental processes and capacities of people who indiscriminately explain a badly sprained ankle, the death of an old man, pneumonia, having one's banana field trampled by an elephant, and a house burning down, by reference to ancestors, ghosts or, above all, witches. But the question misses the point, as it must presume that witchcraft is some substitute for a matter-of-fact explanation; whereas, it is not, being rather a sociological complement of natural cause. It integrates natural cause as it impinges upon the social realm, such as the fire that consumes the house, with the effects within that realm—with *whose* house burned down, or with the destruction of *property*. As such, witchcraft addresses issues for which no people, ourselves included, have any "good" answers, even though the questions, precisely as they are human and not merely "natural" and as they are tragic and not merely empirical, are the most important, the fateful questions: not, "why are you sick?" but "why are *you* sick?"; not, "why did my daughter die in an automobile accident?" but "why *my* daughter?" We speak of chance, accident or the intersection of two autonomous fields of causation. Closer to the primitive, it was bad luck, and closer yet, God's will. The Azande say, "witchcraft":

---

[22] It is beyond even the oracular powers one summons in writing an introductory text to divine an explanation for the series of supernatural variations conjured in this paragraph.

[23] Monica H. Wilson, "Witch Beliefs and Social Structure," *American Journal of Sociology*, LVI (1951), 313.

[24] For a full and unparalleled description of a system of witchcraft and magic, the anthropological classic on witchcraft as an ideology, see E. E. Evans-Pritchard, *Witchcraft, Oracles and Magic Among the Azande* (Oxford: Clarendon Press, 1937).

. . . we shall give a false account of Zande philosophy if we say that they believe witchcraft to be the sole cause of phenomena. This proposition is not contained in Zande patterns of thought, which only assert that witchcraft brings a man into relation with events in such a way that he sustains injury. . . . Fire is hot, but it is not hot owing to witchcraft, for that is its nature. It is a universal quality of fire to burn, but it is not a universal quality of fire to burn *you*. This may never happen; or once in a lifetime, and then only if you have been bewitched.[25]

I return to the general point pursued, that different spirits, as associated with social segments of different order, receive unlike amounts of ritual attention. In the segmentary tribe a regression in cultish practice ordinarily sets in at higher levels, to which corresponds a progressive removal of higher spiritual forces from the here-and-now. But now I would qualify. Under certain circumstances, greater divinities may be invoked by lesser groups, and as it were be thus kept alive. The dialectics of social opposition and integration elicited by ritual action sometimes elicit God. Second, and more important, chiefdom organization reverses the normal segmentary regression of the cult, to rescue God from a premature death.

Ritual action engages persons and groups not only with spirits but with each other in segmentary social relationships. There is, first, a direct or implicit relation of part to whole, segment to tribe. The group may be acting in a matter of autonomous and isolated concern, peculiar to itself, such as its own internal peace or the health of one of its members. The invocation of its own supernatural representation is then altogether fitting. On the other hand, although acting yet on its own behalf, the issue may be of universal (tribal) interest, common to all such groups, such as the growth of crops. Here the ritual group confronts great supernatural agencies in its capacity as a segment of *humanity*. Accordingly, the litany invokes the Great Spirit or the relevant departmental gods, Sun who controls the weather, Earth who nurtures gardens, as well perhaps as the congregation's own tutelary. Second, there is a relation of part to part. Perhaps the supplicants act in their own sectional interest, as opposed to like groups, in an issue of vengeance, for instance. The suitable spirit is then a private patron. On the other hand, the group may act with others in furthering a collective end, or it seeks to establish commonality with others, to repair a breach, make a peace. When Plains Indians' bands gather for the annual tribal hunt, they have a *Sun* Dance. It is essential in such contexts to transcend the private gods whose singular interest in their own devotees is a contradiction to the intent of the ritual and would rob it of integrative function. And if local groups thus met are otherwise autonomous, recognizing no union or collective patron at an intermediate level, there may be nothing for it but to call on the tribal Great Spirit, under whom at least all stand equally subordinate in their common humanity.[26]

In the chiefdom, high god worship is codified and rendered a continuous

---

[25] Evans-Pritchard, *op. cit.*, pp. 68–69. It is impossible to do justice to Evans-Pritchard's examination of the problem with such a snippet as this. Read the book.

[26] The dialectic elicitation of *Kwoth* in different segmentary contexts is described in detail by Evans-Pritchard, "The Nuer Conception of Spirit in Its Relation to the Social Order," pp. 203–209.

fixture. True, the differentiation of kin interests at the base of a segmentary plan persists in all tribal formations, segmentary and chiefdom alike. Personal problems too are eternal, no matter how extensive and integrated the social organism becomes and whatever general problems set in at higher levels. Thus rites and cults of the infrastructure—the homestyle ghost-laying, sorcery, witchcraft, and the like—are not eliminated by greater organization of the tribe. But they are most likely to be added onto, and at times to be submerged by, a collective cult, precisely because the social divisions and oppositions expressed in these practices must be correlated, the part combined in the whole. The decentralized local organization is a refractory basis for higher politics. On the aforementioned principle of mobilizing sacred reserves where secular forces are insufficient, religion is thrown into the political work. Under special conditions (see pp. 12 and 43–44) an important public cult emerges at the village or regional level of a segmentary tribe proper. In the chiefdoms a "national" cult invoking great gods on behalf of chief and chiefdom becomes the rule. God save the chief; alone he might have a difficult time of it. Then again, in a certain historical sense the chief saves God.

The Hawaiians knew sorcery. Sorcerers' powers came from spirits of departed sorcerers and from perfect rendition of the incantations. There were those magicians who prayed a man to death. And there were those who divined the sorcerer and over the corpse of the victim turned back the evil upon its perpetrator—"for a life, a death":

> This is a death I inflict: he is to go and lie in the roadway, and his back split open, a stench arise, and he be devoured by dogs. A death I inflict is to start in him while he is in his own place, and when he goes elsewhere he is to vomit blood, and die, and his grease is to flow on the road, and he be eaten by dogs. . . . This is a death I inflict: he is to fall off a cliff and break his bones, and his grease pour out on the highway. This is a death I inflict: he is to be buried in the earth five *anana* deep, and be dug up by dogs. Such is the death I inflict.[27]

A victim of sorcery might be saved while yet alive by a curer skilled in this practice. Illness caused neither by sorcerers nor by ancestors was treated by practitioners of another kind: medicine men who used simples and herbals, and prayers addressed to deified medicine men and healing gods.

Hairless cannibals lurked in the countryside to waylay travelers at lonely spots. Ghosts frightened people at night. Many of the countless nature sprites were nicer.

Families and apparently larger descent groups as well (*ohana*) had tutelary ancestral spirits (*'aumakua*).[28] The *'aumakua* were revered, rather in a class with Tallensi ancestors than Enga ghosts. They were guardians, benevolent in protecting members of the group from external dangers, rescuing them even from the jaws of death—"a life from the *'aumakua*"—but also punitive as

---

[27] Samuel M. K. Kamakau, *Ka Po'e Kahiko: The People of Old*, Bernice P. Bishop Museum Special Publication 51 (Honolulu: Bishop Museum Press, 1964), 125.

[28] An individual might also have had a particular patron in one of the spirits of his family line.

no mention of the goddesses.

guardians of family virtue, sending illness or worse to those of their line who infringed ritual tabus (*kapu*) or caused harm to kinsmen. If trouble came upon a family by the action of an *'aumakua*, the offended spirit would make himself known through visions or dreams, or through a medium using his own *'aumakua* as a control, and the proper expiation would be likewise revealed. The family gathered then at a certain shrine, a certain stone with attached altar, to make offerings of food and bark cloth to the *'aumakua*. The food was consumed in a solemn feast, evidently a communion with the *'aumakua*. When all this had been done, "no medicine need be given to cure sickness." [29]

Thus within the Hawaiian system, there was a proper and important theology of the lower social levels.

Yet not only that. The stone, phallic in shape, at which families made offerings to their *'aumakua*, was called "the stone of Kane." Here is one link to the theology and cults of the chiefdom level (or of Hawaii as a whole). Kane was first among Hawaiian great gods (*akua*); in relation to the great Ku, Lono, and Kanola, first among equals.[30] But "four-hundred bodied" are the gods. Kane appears also as Kane-the-thunderer (Kanehekili), Kane-breaker-of-the-heavens, Kane-in-the-light, Kane-in-the-dark, and many more Kanes. "There are thousands and thousands of names that are separated into names of the same form. There is only one form, and the names only fit the work done." [31] Now, the guardian *'aumakua* of family lines—as also the tutelaries of occupational pursuits, such as fishing and canoe-building—are identified with these refractions of major gods. Certain ancestors were supposed to have been actually fathered by one or another representation of Kane, Ku, or Lono; other ancestors were apotheosized by dedication to a lesser but still powerful spirit, and transfigured then into a vehicle of that deity (a shark, lightning, a volcanic flame, etc.). Hawaiian theory is complex on this point and sometimes obscure. It is clear, however, that ancestors upon death "entered into" greater spirits, and their powers over descendants came of this godliness. The divinity of ruling chiefs was more direct, genealogically demonstrable: they descended from the gods, Kane particularly. Their status while alive was something of "a refraction on earth," and upon death they were deified by special ritual.

In other words, above and beyond the cult of lower levels was a religion of tribal dimensions, devoted to gods of universal compass—Kane, Ku, Lono and Kanoloa especially. The pivotal human figures in this sphere of cult were ruling chiefs and high priests, and the central places of worship were public

---

[29] Kamakau, *Ka Po'e Kahiko*, p. 33.

[30] This ranking is seen especially in mythology and cultish invocation. In terms of temples and ceremonies at the chiefdom level, however, Ku and Lono seem more central figures (see below).

[31] Kamakau, *op. cit.*, 58. One envisions the following Through-the-Looking-Glass scene:

Hawaiian: We call the name of the god, Kanehekili.
Anthropologist: Oh, Kanehekili is the name of the god.
Hawaiian: Oh no, Kanehekili is just what we call the name of the god. The name of the god is Kane.

The pity is that such a conversation is no longer possible. The literary sources on Hawaiian religion are enigmatic and contradictory at many points. No doubt, first-hand inquiry would have elicited from informants statements just as confusing. The trouble is that there is no way of knowing if the discrepancies in available sources are the same as those informants would have been pleased to produce.

monuments (*heiau*), stone platforms on which were situated various cult-houses and god images.

The life-crisis rites of high-ranking chiefs were public events, marked by ceremonies at main temple-platforms of the chiefdom. Apart from their divine descent, ruling chiefs apparently had special relationships to powerful guardian gods (*akua*). The famous Kamehameha, conqueror of the islands and first king of the post-contact era, was keeper of the image of Kukailimoku, a war god and primary refraction of Ku. The principal temples of a chiefdom were houses of Ku and Lono particularly: Ku, "the god of war and chiefs," and Lono, god of peaceful pursuits, associated with agriculture and fertility. Ku and Lono (at least) had special orders of priesthood devoted to them.[32] These priests presided over the Ku- and Lono-rituals at the greater temples, but shared their privileges with paramount chiefs, to whom fell the right and the obligation to intone certain very sacred prayers.

A lunar month had specified days tabu to Kane, Ku, and other gods, and on these sabbaths religious observance was thus transposed to the tribal level. Periodically too, and especially when contemplating war, a paramount chief would decide to build a special temple to Ku (*luakini heiau*), a process involving human sacrifices, exorbitant offerings, prolonged ceremonies, and the mobilization of the whole people. The whole people also were annually mobilized—or rather immobilized by a tabu on ordinary work—for the great Makahiki, a harvest and renewal ceremony of many weeks' duration (four months, according to most authorities). Here Lono was the central supernatural: his image was carried in procession around an island-chiefdom, watching games and sport in every district and collecting from each place a major first-fruits offering. But the ruling chief was again the central mortal—sharing the food gifts to Lono, incidentally, with the priests.

The support given the chieftainship by the chiefdom-cult is evident in every aspect. And it was evident as well to the chiefs. All native custodians of Hawaiian lore take pains to praise the piety of ruling chiefs. But then, there were definite political advantages. The famous prayer of Liholiho at the temple of Ku:

> O Ku, Kukailimoku,[33] Ku of the bitter path,
> Lononuiakea,[34] Kane and Kanoloa,
> Here are all the offerings before you.
> Curse the rebels without and within
>   who wish to seize the land.
> Grant life to Kamehameha and to all the chiefs,
> To the people in general, the common people,
>   and the Kingdom, from one end to the other, and to me also.[35]
> It is said . . . It is finished.[36]

It is said. It is finished.

---

[32] David Malo, *Hawaiian Antiquities* (Honolulu: Hawaiian Gazette Co., 1903), p. 210.

[33] Kamehameha's war god, refraction of Ku.

[34] Lono in his encompassing aspect (?).

[35] Prayer said on this occasion by Kamehameha's heir, Liholiho.

[36] John Papa Ii, *Fragments of Hawaiian History* Mary Kawena Pukui, trans. (Honolulu: Bishop Museum Press, 1963), p. 37.

Chapter One. For contrasting anthropological views of the "primitive," see Stanley Diamond, "The Search for the Primitive," in I. Gladston, ed., *Man's Image in Medicine and Anthropology* (New York: International Universities Press, 1963), and Francis Hsu, "Rethinking the Concept 'Primitive,'" *Current Anthropology*, V (1964). On the differentiation of civil from primitive society, consult, in addition to Hobbes' *Leviathan* and Rousseau's *Discourse on the Origin of Inequality Among Men*, Frederick Engel's *The Origin of the Family, Private Property and the State* (New York: International Publishers, 1942); Sir Henry Sumner Maine, *Ancient Law* (London: Dent, 1954); "Introduction" by Meyer Fortes and E. E. Evans-Pritchard, eds., *African Political Systems* (London: Oxford University Press, 1940); Morton H. Fried, "Social Stratification and the Evolution of the State," in Stanley Diamond, ed., *Culture and History* (New York: Columbia University Press, 1960); and Leslie A. White, *The Evolution of Culture* (New York: McGraw-Hill, 1959).

Chapter Two. Emile Durkheim's *The Division of Labor in Society* (Chicago: The Free Press, 1947) was the point of departure for anthropological treatments of segmentary societies. British social anthropologists, working on African lineage systems, especially advanced the concept. See Meyer Fortes's summary article, "The Structure of Unilineal Descent Groups," in *American Anthropologist*, LV (1953). A sophisticated theoretical position different from that adopted in this chapter is M. G. Smith, "Segmentary Lineage Systems," *Journal of the Royal Anthropological Institute*, LXXXVI (1956).

Two useful general studies of tribal society are Max Gluckman, *Politics, Law and Ritual in Tribal Society* (Chicago: Aldine, 1965), and Elman R. Service, *Primitive Social Organization* (New York: Random House, 1962).

Chapter Three. See June Helm's review, "The Ecological Approach in Anthropology," *American Journal of Sociology*, LXVII (1962). Harold C. Conklin provides an extensive bibliography on swiddening in "The Study of Shifting Cultivation," *Current Anthropology*, II (1961). On animal husbandry and pastoral nomadism, see the works by Barth, Krader, and Lattimore cited in the text, and also, Anthony Leeds and Andrew P. Vayda, eds., *Man, Culture, and Animals* (Washington, D. C.: American Association for the Advancement of Science, 1965). For an ethnographic treatment of a hunting-gathering tribe, consult Philip Drucker, *The Northern and Central Nootkan Tribes*, Smithsonian Institution, Bureau of American Ethnology, Bull. 144 (Washington, D. C.: Government Printing Office, 1951); of an equestrian-hunting tribe, Robert Lowie, *The Crow Indians* (New York: Rinehart, 1955); of Pueblo agriculturalists, M. Titiev, "Old Oraibi," *Papers of the Peabody Museum of American Archaeology and Ethnology*, XXII (1944). For bibliographic leads to Melanesia and Polynesia, see Douglas Oliver, *The Pacific Islands* (Garden City: Doubleday Anchor and American Museum of Natural History, 1961).

Chapter Four. John Barnes' article, "Kinship," in *The Encyclopaedia Brittanica* (1964) is a useful introduction to the subject. The following exemplify several main anthropological approaches to the study of primitive social organization: "functionalist," A. R. Radcliffe-Brown, *Structure and Function in Primitive Society* (Glencoe, Ill.: The Free Press, 1952); "cross-cultural inductionist," George P. Murdock, *Social Structure* (New York: Macmillan, 1949); "structuralist," Claude Lévi-Strauss, *Les Structures Elémentaires de la Parenté* (Paris: Presses Universitaires de France, 1949); "evolutionist," Elman R. Service, *Primitive Social Organization* (New York: Random House, 1962); "cognitive," E. A. Hammel, ed., "Formal Semantic Analysis," *Special Publication, American Anthropologist*, LXVII (1965).

For an ethnography of a conical clan system, see Raymond Firth, *We, The Tikopia* (London: Allen and Unwin, 1957); a segmentary lineage system, E. E. Evans-Pritchard, *The Nuer* (Oxford: Clarendon Press,/1940); territorial clans, Mervyn Meggitt, *The Lineage System of the Mae Enga of New Guinea* (Edinburgh: Oliver and Boyd, 1965); dispersed clans, Douglas Oliver, *A Solomon Islands Society* (Cambridge, Mass.: Harvard University Press, 1955). See also, Morton H. Fried, "The Classification of Unilineal Descent Groups," *Journal of the Royal Anthropological Institute*, LXXXVII (1957).

Special topics treated in this chapter may be further pursued in Rodney Needham, *Structure and Sentiment* (Chicago: University of Chicago Press, 1962)—on unilateral cross-cousin marriage; D. M. Schneider and Kathleen Gough, eds., *Matrilineal Kinship* (Berkeley and Los Angeles: University of California Press, 1961); A. R. Radcliffe-Brown and D. Forde, eds., *African Systems of Kinship and Marriage* and C. Lévi-Strauss, "The Family" in H. Shapiro, ed., *Man, Culture, and Society* (New York: Oxford University Press, 1960); E. R. Leach, "Concerning Trobriand Clans and the Kinship Category *Tabu*," in J. Goody, ed., *The Developmental Cycle in Domestic Groups* (Cambridge: Cambridge University Press, 1958); A. M. Hocart, "Kinship Systems," in J. P. Jennings and E. A. Hoebel, eds., *Readings in Anthropology* (New York: McGraw-Hill, 1966).

Chapter Five. "Economic Anthropology" is currently beset by controversy between those (the "substantivists") who oppose the application of formal economic theory to primitive economies, and those (the "formalists") who advocate it. My own treatment has been in the substantivist vein. For the latest formalist rebuttal, containing also a bibliography of the controversy, see Scott Cook, "The Obsolete 'Anti-Market' Mentality," *American Anthropologist*, LXVIII (1966).

A useful summary is C. Daryll Forde and Mary Douglas, "Primitive Economics," in H. Shapiro, ed., *Man, Culture, and Society* (New York: Oxford University Press, 1960). Outstanding monographic treatments include Bronislaw Malinowski, *Argonauts of the Western Pacific* (London: Routledge and Kegan Paul, 1922); Raymond Firth, *Primitive Polynesian Economy* (London: Routledge and Kegan Paul, 1965); R. F. Salisbury, *From Stone to Steel* (New York: Cambridge University Press, 1962).

Chapter Six. See E. E. Evans-Pritchard, *Theories of Primitive Religion* (Oxford: Clarendon Press, 1965), for a critical exposition of traditional perspectives.

In addition to ethnographic accounts in the text, see John Middleton, *Lugbara Religion* (London: Oxford University Press, 1960); Reo Fortune, *Manus Religion* (Philadelphia: American Philosophical Society, 1935); Clyde Kluckhohn, "Navaho Witchcraft," *Papers of the Peabody Museum of American Archaeology and Ethnology*, XXII (1944); W. A. Lessa and E. Z. Vogt, eds., *Reader in Comparative Religion* (Evanston: Row, Peterson, 1958); Charles Leslie, ed., *Anthropology of Folk Religion* (New York: Vintage, 1960); Claude Lévi-Strauss, *Totemism* (Boston: Beacon, 1963).

DATE DUE

JAN. 2 4 1985			
GAYLORD			PRINTED IN U.S.A.